TODD WILBUR'S TOP SECRET RECIPES ARE THE CRITICS' FAVORITE DISH!

"There's something almost magically compelling about the idea of making such foods at home.... The allure is undeniable, and stuffed with tidbits and lore you're unlikely to find anywhere else."
—*Boston Herald*

"This is the cookbook to satisfy all your cravings."
—Juli Huss, author of *The Faux Gourmet*

"The mission: Decode the secret recipes for America's favorite junk foods. Equipment: Standard kitchen appliance. Goal: Leak the results to a ravenous public."
—*USA Today*

TODD WILBUR is the author of *Top Secret Recipes*, *More Top Secret Recipes*, and *Top Secret Restaurant Recipes* (all available from Plume). When not taste-testing recipes on himself, his friends, or TV talk-show hosts, Todd lives in Las Vegas, Nevada.

ALSO BY TODD WILBUR

Top Secret Recipes
More Top Secret Recipes
Top Secret Restaurant Recipes

TOP SECRET RECIPES

LITE!

Creating Reduced-Fat
Kitchen Clones of America's
Favorite Brand-Name Foods

TODD WILBUR

With Illustrations by the Author

A PLUME BOOK

PLUME
Published by the Penguin Group
Penguin Putnam Inc., 375 Hudson Street, New York, New York 10014, U.S.A.
Penguin Books Ltd, 27 Wrights Lane, London W8 5TZ, England
Penguin Books Australia Ltd, Ringwood, Victoria, Australia
Penguin Books Canada Ltd, 10 Alcorn Avenue, Toronto, Ontario, Canada M4V 3B2
Penguin Books (N.Z.) Ltd, 182–190 Wairau Road, Auckland 10, New Zealand

Penguin Books Ltd, Registered Offices: Harmondsworth, Middlesex, England

First published by Plume, a member of Penguin Putnam Inc.

First Printing, November, 1998
10   9   8   7   6   5   4   3

To the best of the author's knowledge, the information regarding company backgrounds and product histories is true and accurate. Any misrepresentation of factual material is completely unintentional.

CIP is available.
ISBN: 0-452-28014-1

Printed in the United States of America
Set in Gill Sans Light and Gill Sans Regular

To radio gods, Don & Mike—
m'boys, m'boys!

THANK YOU...

Everyone at Penguin Putnam for helping to make the
TSR books a success
Marilyn Hart and Kate Baltz for your
fabulous assistance in the kitchen
Lori Lipsky, Editor in Chief extraordinaire
Kimberly Perdue, assistant editor extraordinaire
Gus Samios, attorney extraordinaire
My supporting family and friends
All fat replacement products
Zebu, the Floormat (formerly the Wonder Dog)
Beer

CONTENTS

TOP SECRET RECIPES—LITE! CONVERSIONS

INTRODUCTION

Before I begin, let me assure you that my love for the gooey, greasy, cheesy, sugary, sloppy, slippery, creamy, saucy, and chocolaty famous American convenience foods cloned in previous *Top Secret Recipes* books has not diminished in the least. I'm still in ecstasy when sinking my teeth into a hot double-stacked burger slathered in secret sauce, or when chomping down hard into a chocolate bar loaded with caramel, nougat, and a fistful of nuts.

I don't care who you are, or how healthy you claim to eat, or how much you boast you never divert your car in a rush through a fast-food drive-thru joint for a quickie. It's a sure bet that you have at least one favorite, sinfully delicious food that you often crave, that's high in fat and calories. I'm talking about the kind of food that gives you an ecstatic rush as you eat it, and practically gets you high from the oral gratification. I'm talking about the type of grub that washes over your tastebuds in that all-too-short belly-stuffing journey, making you close your eyes for just a moment while you chew to let out a little "mmmm." It's the euphoric palatal experience that ends much too soon. And it's the experience that's quickly followed by the post-nosh guilt, as you realize the pants are a bit more snug today, and will be a lot more snug tomorrow.

Sure, I still enjoy eating America's favorite brand-name foods, and I still dig cloning them at home, just as much as ever. But I also realize that no matter how good the stuff tastes, these higher-fat foods can't be on the menu every day if I want to maintain a 6-foot-tall, 180-pound frame. Sure, if I gave in to my cravings, I'd be eating huge portions of Olive Garden Tiramisu, Taco Bell Mexican Pizza, KFC Cole Slaw, and Big Mac after Big Mac (I'll have fries with that, please). And I could eat Hooters Buffalo Wings every day of the year and not get sick of them ... until around Thanksgiving. Okay, make that Christmas.

But I don't pig out wildly on these foods because I know that, while these products are delicious and popular, some of them contain significant amounts of fat. And we've all been informed by the scads of nutritionists and dieticians on anti-fat crusades that if we want to stay fit, we're going to have to turn away from the greasy goodies and start looking in the direction of "low-fat alternatives." I've heard it, you've heard it; and as much as I don't want to hear it anymore, I know I will, and so will you. And the real bummer is, it's all true.

This news was even more of a bummer in the early days of the move away from foods higher in fat. Back then, smart, tasty alternatives were hard to come by. Food manufacturers were coming out with products that tasted only slightly better than potting soil. Maybe that's why when we hear the words "low-fat" or "fat-free" today, while we know it's the right thing to choose, a part of us is thinking "yech!"

But the good news is that in the last several years, fat-reduced foods have been much improved. There are many more better-tasting staple products such as mayonnaise, cheese, sour cream, and butter-flavored additives available than ever before. With these products and the skillful use of thickeners, starches, and fruit purees, it's now easier to enjoy foods that taste as though they're pumped with fat, when the nutrition facts say otherwise. The tricks we're learning to remove the fat from our meals and snacks, both in the food production plants and in the home kitchens, are quickly turning the "yechs" into "yums."

As I was creating the previous *Top Secret Recipes* books, I began to devise simple ways to use lower-fat ingredients and special cooking techniques that would eliminate much of the fat, yet retain the flavor of the original product. This was a casual exercise, for my own meals, and I was at first only moderately effective. But as I explored and experimented further over the years, and started to use the many new fat-free ingredients that were becoming available, I found that it was possible to eliminate at least 50 percent of the fat in most cloned convenience foods, with minimal effort and standard ingredients. The big surprise was that in many cases I could get the fat down much lower than that—as low as 15 to 20 percent of the original product.

Isn't it amazing that only twenty-five years ago we could eat the same higher-fat foods available today without feeling that we had done something horribly wrong. Today we still have the same classic burgers, famous fried food, top-selling candy bars, snack cakes, and cookies that have been around for years; and these items are as popular as ever. But in this last decade of the millennium we are continuously force-fed information about what is good and bad for our bodies. How often have you heard that we should eat no more than 2200 calories a day and that we should limit our fat intake to around 60 grams? Sure we hear it, and we know it. But that information doesn't keep us from loving our favorite junk foods. It just makes us feel much worse when we cave in.

Food manufacturers are aware of our dilemma, and they realize that creating products that address our nutritional concerns *and* that satisfy our strongest, most insatiable cravings, is a quick trip down mega-profits street. Millions and millions of dollars have been spent on reduced-fat product development, and for conversion of previously higher-fat products to trendy lower-fat versions. Just look for the green packages. Not only can these healthier alternatives be found in growing numbers in supermarket aisles, but also fast-food outlets and restaurant chains have been making lower-fat choices available. It's the latest food craze, and the cost to the consumer is usually high. Ironically, many times the lower-fat or light versions of a product are more expensive or smaller in size (or both) than the higher-fat counterpart.

And as these food companies with their "healthy alternatives" are wrestling for shelf space and customers, scores of cookbook authors have jumped into the fray. Low-fat cookbooks have been some of the most popular books sold in recent years, with some scoring high on bestseller lists. Many of these books have some great ideas and delicious recipes (and some definitely don't), but not one gives us recipes for the type of food for which we really want homemade reduced-fat versions. I'm talking about the kind of food that sales figures show is the most popular food—convenience food, fast food, and junk food. America's favorite foods.

If you are discouraged to find that supermarkets are filled with record numbers of overly expensive and not-so-fresh low-fat products; or if you have wished for reduced-fat versions of your favorite brand-name foods; or if you have yearned for a low-fat cookbook that actually provides recipes to make dishes at home that taste good rather than tasting low-fat, then I'm hoping to make your day.

This book will show you how to make low-fat and fat-free food at home that will taste just like these reduced-fat products you find in restaurants and supermarkets, at a fraction of the cost. At the same time, this book will show you how to cook reduced-fat food at home that tastes as good as the popular brands that're usually higher in fat.

TWO, TWO, TWO BOOKS IN ONE

What you have here is like two books in one. The first section is a collection of recipes that taste like existing low-fat and fat-free products. These are famous products such as Nabisco Snack-Well's Cookies, Weight Watchers Éclairs, Hostess Lights Twinkies, Kellogg's Low-Fat Pop-Tarts, and Gardenburger Veggie Patties. These products are created by the manufacturers as lower-fat versions of their existing higher-fat products, or as an entirely new line of products created solely for the fat-conscious eaters. Some of these products, such as Einstein Bros. Bagels, are just naturally low in fat, without much attention drawn to that fact.

When creating these clone recipes for the products in the first half of the book, I've made every attempt to keep fat gram numbers the same as the real item. This was not always easy. In fact, it was rarely easy, and next to the boxes, cans, and bottles of ingredients on the kitchen counter could always be found a well-stained calculator, ready to spew running fat totals.

With the recipes in the first half of the book, you can now

recreate your favorite low-fat and fat-free foods with everyday ingredients. This gives you the opportunity to enjoy a product that may not be available where you live, and, in most cases, you will find that creating the product at home from scratch saves a significant amount of money, versus buying the real thing. Plus fresh food is always better than the packaged stuff, which may contain preservatives.

The second section is the fat-reduction extravaganza. This part of the book is filled with recipes to clone items that don't exist as lower-fat or fat-free food. I call these recipes "TSR Lite Conversions," and it is here where you will find recipes to recreate America's favorite brand-name foods, but with significantly reduced numbers in the fat column. Every recipe reduces the fat grams by at least 50 percent when compared to the original product—and in many cases, by significantly more than that.

The recipes in this section make it possible for you to get lower-fat versions of products that would otherwise be impossible to enjoy. With these recipes you can now have a cinnamon roll that tastes like Cinnabon Cinnamon Rolls with only 4 grams of fat, while the actual product contains 24 grams of fat. You can savor the flavor of Boston Market's Creamed Spinach for just one-fourth the fat grams (6g fat) of the original (24g fat). You can eat two clone hamburgers (13g fat each) with the same taste of a Big Mac, but still not consume as much fat as just one of the real burgers (31g fat).

Here are some other examples of the incredible fat savings when compared to the original:

	Original	TSR Conversion
Burger King BK Broiler	29 grams	6 grams
Chi-Chi's "Fried" Ice Cream	34 grams (est.)	7 grams
Hooters Buffalo Wings	30 grams (est.)	10 grams
KFC Buttermilk Biscuits	10 grams	2.5 grams
McDonald's Breakfast Burrito	19 grams	2.5 grams
Olive Garden Tiramisu	38 grams (est.)	2.9 grams
Otis Spunkmeyer Banana Nut Muffins	12 grams	5 grams

	Original	TSR Conversion
Red Lobster Cheddar Biscuits	7 grams	3 grams
Shoney's Country Fried Steak	37 grams	10 grams
Taco Bell Mexican Pizza	36 grams	10 grams
Wendy's Frosty	11 grams	2 grams

There are even several TSR conversions that cut out all the fat. With these recipes you can now enjoy fat-free versions of Olive Garden's Italian Salad Dressing, Boston Market Butternut Squash, and Red Lobster Tartar Sauce. And even though KFC's famous cole slaw contains more than 10 grams of fat per serving, you now have a TSR conversion to recreate a fat-free clone—and it's made with only five ingredients!

THE TOP SECRET TRICKS

As I created the recipes in previous *Top Secret Recipes* books, I gave priority to one very important guideline: All ingredients for the recipes must be available in the local supermarket. This is often difficult, as manufacturers love to pack their ingredients list with additives, flavorings, stabilizers, and preservatives with long names that consumers like you and me will never be able to track down at the neighborhood Safeway. We must then find substitutes for the commercial components, while dismissing preservatives entirely, since our homemade versions won't be sitting on the shelves for weeks at a time. I would hope.

Adhering to this rule presented a bigger challenge than ever when creating these reduced-fat recipes. That's because in the low-fat and fat-free food manufacturing world, companies use obscure gums and thickeners and modified starches to replace the missing fat in their products. These additional ingredients are necessary to give a product the textural qualities of fat. Although carrageenan, xanthan gum, cellulose gel, and carob bean gum are missing from supermarket aisles, we do have access to many products that can stand in nicely. The trick is in determining the best ingredient for each situation. Lots of time is logged over a stovetop and mixing bowl figuring out if a recipe works better with pectin or gelatin or cornstarch or arrowroot, or other available thickeners and additives that may help to give the finished product a pleasant texture.

A baked product may be best with some fruit puree mixed in. Raisin or prune or banana purees lend a nice flavor to cakes and brownies and cookies, and they help a snack retain moisture and give it a pleasant, chewy consistency. Unsweetened applesauce can make magic happen. And sweetened condensed skim milk works great with its sweet fat-free gooeyness.

In creamy sauces and dressings, we might use fat-free versions of sour cream, mayonnaise, strained nonfat yogurt, cream cheese, or evaporated milk. For creamy desserts, fat-free puddings and Dream Whip come in very handy.

Also included in our arsenal will be products to replace the butter in many of the recipes. Fleischmann's Fat Free Buttery Spread, I Can't Believe It's Not Butter Spray, and Butter Buds Sprinkles are excellent weapons in the TSR fight against fat.

I've even made a special effort to find substitutes for soy lecithin and whey, common in baked goods, but only available in health food stores. Even though some low-fat cookbooks include these items in their recipes, I felt that they were not common enough to include. You will also find that I leave in some optional suggestions for ingredients, such as cake decorating items like clear vanilla, brown paste food coloring, and meringue powder, but that these are not necessary to complete the recipe. They are only suggested to make a better clone. There is, however, one case where bulgur wheat is essential. That's in the *Top Secret Recipes* version of the Gardenburger Original Veggie Patty. You just can't create that one without bulgur wheat, which you can sometimes find in supermarkets (it's becoming increasingly more popular), but in many cities may require a trip to the health food store.

Prepare to have several of these ingredients on hand as you go forth into the world of lower-fat kitchen cloning.

While these ingredients help greatly in our fight against fat, there are a great many tricks that involve the cooking process itself. In some recipes, for example, we'll leave the skin on chicken pieces while they bake to lock in the juiciness, then we'll strip it off during the final cooking stages. And we'll recreate fried products such as Shoney's Country Fried Steak and Hooters Buffalo Chicken Wings by breading the meat and spraying it with a light coating of vegetable oil cooking spray before baking the portions in a very hot oven.

By using this book, you'll surely learn to use some ingredients and cooking techniques that will help you reduce the fat from many of your own favorite recipes. And food companies will surely continue to develop additional ingredients in the future that will further add to your personal reduced-fat cooking bag of tricks.

A TRIBUTE TO OUR GOOD FRIEND, MR. FAT

Most of us remember a time when we ate only for taste, with little regard for ingredients and cooking methods. Only a dozen or so years ago much of our food was fried in animal tallow. Butter, heavy cream, and oil were added to foods indiscriminately, in large amounts. Eggs were eaten every morning, and red meat every night. Then a little ice cream would be thrown in for dessert.

After all, this is America, a supreme technologically advanced superpower, land of the free, home of the brave, and the world's fattest nation. It's the country where the average citizen eats 130 pounds of fat per year, or the equivalent of a stick of butter every day. This is the country where, according to Joseph Piscatella in *Choices for a Healthy Heart*, "the typical adult American male weighs 20 to 30 pounds too much, and the typical female is overweight by 15 to 30 pounds."

Even though there are entire areas of the globe where coronary heart disease is not known, obesity is the American way. But it's a recent problem that goes back not as far as you might think. Prior to World War II, Americans were primarily blue-collar laborers, working hard in factories, burning off massive amounts of calories, and staying lean. Like professional athletes, these workers could eat large amounts of food and, as fuel, it would burn off with the daily activity.

But after the war, automation eased the workloads. The country began a shift to a more white-collar society working to process the increasing amounts of information. Modern-day conveniences were being developed to make life easier. Automobile sales were skyrocketing and television became America's favorite leisure-time activity.

These developments were the beginning of our nation's new sedentary lifestyle. The fat and calories that were once burned off were just sitting there as folks leisurely rested in a car every day while driving to work and then, at the office, sat for many hours behind a desk. Back home, after sitting again for dinner, more sitting was still to come in front of the tube until bedtime. Sitting upon sitting upon sitting, without adjustments to the heavy diets, led to the inevitable consequences: millions of cases of obesity, high cholesterol, and coronary heart disease. This was not a good thing.

To make matters worse, after the war many soldiers returning from overseas wanted the luxury of gourmet meals smothered in thick creamy sauces, butter and cheese, and entrées of red meat. These thick greasy ingredients became known as luxury items and were much sought after at the time, especially for those who had been denied them for so long. It would eventually become clear that our diets would have to change.

Millions of heart attacks later, in the 1980s, the tide was turning as growing numbers of Americans began to heed the advice of the dieticians who had been emphasizing the need to cut down on the fat choking off our precious arteries. They told us that while our bodies do need some fat to function, too much of the stuff leads to high cholesterol and coronary heart disease. They told us that the body is limited in the amount of proteins and carbohydrates it stores, but there is no limit to the amount of fat it can accumulate.

It was in the late eighties that the increasing interest to reduce the fat in our foods began to show up in numerous products on grocery store shelves. But, it wasn't until the 1990s that the trend really took off.

The three words "Reduced in Fat" became the most appealing descriptor for products in supermarkets. Slapping the words "low-fat" or "fat-free" on the products, and using green on the packaging to indicate reduced fat, maintained brand loyalty and kept the customers in a manufacturer's corner. Those who held out converting their brands in the earliest part of the decade would eventually give in to create low-fat clones of their existing products as well. The low-fat rush was on.

Consumers demanded low-fat alternatives like never before. Just look at the trend: In 1994, there were 70 percent more reduced-fat products than in the year before. In 1995, that number went up again, to 1,914 new products. In 1996, it was up again, to 2,076. And today this number continues to climb.

At this rate, we'll exit this last decade of the millennium with green as the most commonly used color on product packaging in supermarket aisles. And that trend will continue to grow as scientists perfect magical new fat replacers that will allow us to eat formerly higher-fat foods without digesting a single gram—the fat will just pass right through. Newfangled substitutes, like Olestra and Salatrim, are now being marketed in snack food production by companies such as Nabisco, Frito-Lay, and Hershey. And you can expect to hear much more about these and other fat replacers in the near future; and about new developments on the horizon, such as a way to coat french fries with pectin to keep the oil from soaking in.

Yes, the low-fat revolution is on. And, with so many products to choose from, consumers are finding they can now limit the amount of fat in their diet and satisfy their cravings. The best of both worlds.

I'VE GOT YOUR LABEL RIGHT HERE

In 1990, when the Food and Drug Administration passed laws that standardized labeling of nutrition information on all products, confusion over what our food was offering us in regard to fat and calories came to an end. Or did it?

Prior to 1990, nutrition labeling was required only of products that had added nutrients or when nutrition claims appeared on the label. Cereals fortified with "8 essential vitamins and minerals" were to list those extra nutrients and include the percentage of daily recommended allowance satisfied by a single serving.

Today, in addition to Daily Value percentages, the labels are printed in large, easy-to-read type, with the heading "Nutrition Facts." Manufacturers are required to list calories, fat, saturated fat, cholesterol, fibers, sodium, and several other important nutritional contents on a per serving measurement.

Serving sizes must closely reflect the amount people eat (although that's certainly open for debate), and similar products must measure the same amount for nutritional analysis. For example, each brand of cookies measures approximately 1 ounce for analysis, for salad dressing it's 2 tablespoons, and for ice cream it's ½ cup.

One of the most misunderstood and confusing labeling practices concerns the fat claims now splashed across the front of product packages to encourage sales. There is much confusion about the combinations of two words, of which one is always "fat." "Reduced-Fat," "Low-Fat," "Fat-Free": Each of these terms means something different. Then, when we throw "Light," "Lean," and "Extra Lean" into the mix, it can all become a bit confusing.

Allow me to shed some light:

Reduced-Fat: This means that the product has at least 25 percent less fat per serving than the original food. Reduced-Fat Nabisco Cheese Nips have 3.5 grams of fat per serving, whereas the original full-fat Cheese Nips contain 6 grams of fat per serving.

Low-Fat: The product must contain 3 grams of fat or less per serving. The Reduced-Fat Cheese Nips mentioned above don't quite qualify as low-fat—they're ½ gram too heavy. However, Nabisco Reduced Fat 'Nilla Wafers (2 grams of fat per serving) qualify for the "low-fat" label. Nevertheless, Nabisco chose to go with "Reduced Fat." (Probably to stay consistent with its other products.)

Fat-Free: While you may assume that a product must contain no fat at all to qualify for this label, that is not entirely true. Adding up all of the fat grams contained within one package of a "fat-free" product might indeed reveal dozens of grams of fat. To qualify as "fat-free" a product is required to contain less than ½ a gram of fat *per serving.* An entire jar of fat-free mayonnaise may contain a total of 30 grams of fat, but since it holds 64 servings, with each serving under ½ gram of fat, the mayo is still considered "fat-free."

Light: This one means two things, and can be misleading.

Either the food must have one-third fewer calories or half the fat of the referenced food, or it means that a low-fat or low-calorie food has a sodium content that is reduced by half of the referenced food. Read the label carefully to determine exactly what "light" is referring to.

"Lite!" as it is used in the title of this book, refers to the low-fat claims of the original products cloned in the first section. For the second section, it refers to the amount by which the recipes have been reduced in fat—at least 50 percent.

Low-Calorie: The product has no more than 40 calories per serving.

Calorie-Free: The product has less than 5 calories per serving.

Lean: Found on meat packaging, this means that the product has less than 10 grams of total fat per serving.

Extra Lean: Also found on meat packaging, this means that the product has less than 5 grams of total fat per serving.

David Lean: Directed the movie *Lawrence of Arabia.* Rarely used.

All of the rules that apply to the labels on the food you find in your supermarket are used in the same manner within this book. If the recipe says "*Top Secret Recipes* Low-Fat version of Taco Bell Beef Soft Taco" you can expect a serving of the finished product to have 3 grams of fat or less.

SPECIAL AUTHOR'S NOTE

The nutritional facts (fat and calories) included with each of the clone recipes were compiled with the help of manufacturers' labels, and fat gram and calorie content reference material. Care was taken to make very accurate calculations, but these numbers can vary slightly from brand to brand for certain ingredients. In these cases I used the numbers from the most popular brands available.

Most of the fat and calorie information for the manufacturers' original products comes from that company's printed nutritional information materials produced by corporate offices. Any nutrition information that was not available was calculated based on full-fat versions of the low-fat clone recipe. When these are estimated figures, I have indicated so.

As with my other books, none of these recipes has been created with the cooperation of the manufacturers. No manufacturers have endorsed this work, but I thank each and every one of them for creating the great food that has become so popular as to warrant its inclusion here.

Please know that I did not swipe, heist, or bribe, or otherwise obtain any formulas through coercion or illegal means. However I do admit to occasionally kidnapping samples of the restaurant food in doggie bags (after paying for them, of course), and transporting it to my hardly secret laboratory for further examination and experimentation.

While the product dissections may have appeared cruel, I assure you that no foodstuffs were harmed in the creation of this book.

SO LET'S GET COOKING!

Now, if you're ready to munch out on some fat-saving clones, get out some ingredients and measuring spoons, and tie on that apron. Or, better yet, start being really, really nice to the person you intend to persuade to do all of the cooking for you.

Whoever decides to give these recipes a try will find the recipes easy to follow, even for the novice chef. So dive right in, and get ready to enjoy lower-fat clones that are so good you don't even miss the fat.

If you'd like some more kitchen clone recipes, be sure to check out the other *Top Secret Recipes* books, also from Plume.

You may also want to surf on over to the official Web site, *Top Secret Recipes on the Web,* for dozens more recipes you won't find anywhere else, and new weekly content:

http://www.topsecretrecipes.com

If you have suggestions for recipes to clone in future *Top Secret Recipes* books, drop me a note at:

Todd Wilbur—Top Secret Recipes
c/o Penguin Putnam Inc.
375 Hudson Street
New York, NY 10014-3657

Or send e-mail to:

Todd@topsecretrecipes.com

Until next time, happy cloning!

—Todd Wilbur

TOP SECRET RECIPES *LITE!* **CLONES**

APPLEBEE'S LOW-FAT BLACKENED CHICKEN SALAD

The big secret to keeping a tasty salad low in fat is to develop a dressing that's low in fat, or even better, fat-free. This recipe clones one of Applebee's most popular low-fat dishes from its "Low-Fat and Fabulous" selections. It's one dish that customers have raved about, because it's so delicious it just doesn't seem possible it could contain only 7 grams of fat. The burst of flavor from the marinated and blackened chicken helps to hide the lack of fat. And the dressing, which is made so incredibly light by using a fat-free mayonnaise base, is indescribably delicious.

DRESSING

1/4 cup fat-free mayonnaise
1/4 cup Grey Poupon Dijon
    mustard
1 tablespoon prepared mustard

1/4 cup honey
1 tablespoon white vinegar
1/8 teaspoon paprika

CHICKEN MARINADE

1 cup water
3 tablespoons lime juice
2 tablespoons soy sauce

1/2 tablespoon Worcestershire
    sauce

2 chicken breast fillets

CAJUN SPICE BLEND

½ tablespoon salt

1 teaspoon sugar

1 teaspoon paprika

1 teaspoon onion powder

1 teaspoon black pepper

½ teaspoon garlic powder

½ teaspoon cayenne pepper

½ teaspoon white pepper

½ tablespoon butter

SALAD

8 cups chopped iceberg lettuce

½ cup shredded red cabbage

½ cup shredded carrot

½ cup shredded fat-free mozzarella cheese

½ cup shredded fat-free cheddar cheese

1 hard-boiled egg white, diced

1 large tomato, diced

1. Make the dressing by first combining the mayonnaise with the mustards in a small bowl. Whisk thoroughly until the ingredients are well combined. Mix in the honey, then the vinegar and paprika. Store the dressing in a covered container in the refrigerator until the salads are ready.

2. Combine the water, lime juice, soy sauce, and Worcestershire in a medium bowl, and stir. Add the chicken fillets to the marinade, cover the bowl, and keep it in the refrigerator for several hours. Marinate the chicken overnight, if you've got the time.

3. When the chicken is well marinated, preheat a frying pan or skillet (an iron skillet, if you've got it) over medium/high heat. Also, preheat your barbecue grill to medium/high heat.

4. Combine the spices for the Cajun spice blend in a small bowl. Sprinkle a teaspoon of the spice blend over one side of each chicken fillet. Cover the entire top surface of the chicken with an even coating of the spice blend.

5. Melt the butter in the hot pan, then sauté the chicken fillets for 2 to 3 minutes on the side with the spices. While the first side cooks, sprinkle another teaspoon of spice over the top of each chicken breast, coating that side as you did the other. Flip the chicken over, and sauté for another 2 to 3 minutes. The surface

of the chicken should end up with a charred-looking black coating.

6. Finish the chicken off on your barbecue grill. Grill each breast on both sides for 2 to 3 minutes, or until done.

7. While the chicken is cooking, prepare the salads by splitting the lettuce into two large bowls. Toss in the red cabbage and carrots. Mix the cheeses together, then top the salad with the cheese blend and hard-boiled egg white. Sprinkle half of the diced tomato over each salad.

8. Slice the chicken breasts crosswise to ½-inch-thick pieces. Spread the chicken over the top of the salads and serve immediately with dressing on the side.

• Serves 2 as an entrée.

Nutrition Facts

Serving size—1 salad
Total servings—2

Fat (per serving)—7g
Calories (per serving)—420

• • • •

APPLEBEE'S LOW-FAT VEGGIE QUESADILLA

The menu description's got the scoop: "Fresh mushrooms, red pepper, onion, broccoli, & carrots smothered in nonfat shredded Cheddar/Mozzarella blend & sandwiched between two wheat tortillas. Served with fat-free sour cream & shredded lettuce. Less than 10 grams of fat."

The TSR version of this tasty favorite appetizer comes in with a fat gram count that's even slightly lower than that, at only 6 grams. The fat-free cheese is where you're spared the major fat gram dosage. And the fat-free sour cream on the side, which nicely completes this guilt-free veggie-filled finger food, certainly helps to keep the waistline in check.

½ tablespoon canola oil
½ cup sliced mushrooms
⅓ cup shredded carrot
⅓ cup chopped broccoli
2 tablespoons diced onion
1 tablespoon diced red bell
    pepper
1 teaspoon soy sauce
dash cayenne pepper

dash black pepper
dash salt
2 10-inch whole wheat flour
    tortillas
¼ cup shredded fat-free cheddar
    cheese
¼ cup shredded fat-free
    mozzarella cheese
nonstick cooking spray

ON THE SIDE
fat-free sour cream
Pace picante salsa

shredded lettuce

1. In a frying pan that has a bigger diameter than the tortillas, sauté the vegetables in the oil over medium/high heat for 5 to 7 minutes. Season with soy sauce, peppers, and salt.
2. Pour the vegetables into a bowl, and place the frying pan back on the heat, but reduce the heat to medium/low.
3. Place one of the tortillas in the pan, and sprinkle half of the cheeses on the tortilla. Spread the vegetables over the cheese, then sprinkle the rest of the cheeses over the vegetables. Put the second tortilla on top, and cook for 1 to 2 minutes, or until heated through and the cheese is melted. Flip the quesadilla over and cook for 1 to 2 more minutes.
4. Slide the quesadilla onto a cutting board and slice it like a pizza into 6 equal pieces. Serve hot with fat-free sour cream, salsa, and shredded lettuce on the side.

- SERVES 2 AS AN APPETIZER.

Nutrition Facts

SERVING SIZE—½ QUESADILLA	FAT (PER SERVING)—6G
TOTAL SERVINGS—2	CALORIES (PER SERVING)—274

• • • •

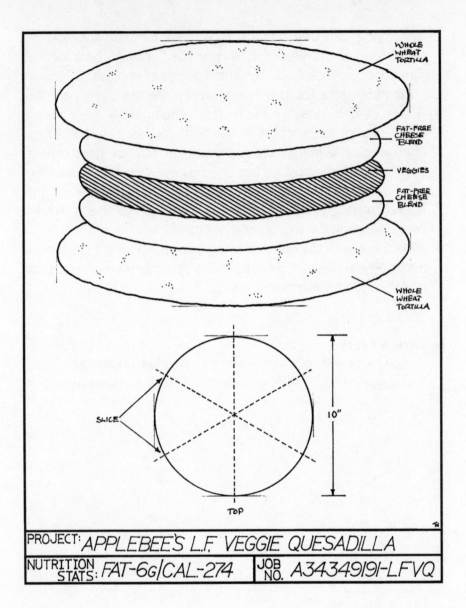

WHOLE WHEAT TORTILLA

FAT-FREE CHEESE BLEND

VEGGIES

FAT-FREE CHEESE BLEND

WHOLE WHEAT TORTILLA

SLICE

10"

TOP

PROJECT: *APPLEBEE'S L.F. VEGGIE QUESADILLA*

NUTRITION STATS: *FAT-6G/CAL.-274*

JOB NO. *A34349191-LFVQ*

ARBY'S LIGHT MENU ROAST CHICKEN DELUXE

Here's an awesome kitchen clone for a selection off of Arby's 3-item "Light Menu." As other fast food chains were zigging by creating giant gooey burgers with fat grams in the 40-plus range, this 3,100-outlet roast beef sandwich chain opted to zag, offering a selection of scrumptious sandwiches with only 6 to 10 grams of fat each.

The secret to recreating the special Arby's taste in the Roast Chicken Deluxe is in the marinade. Let your chicken soak in it for several hours, or even overnight, if you've got the patience. It also helps if you have a meat slicer to get that paper-thin, deli-style cut to the chicken. If you don't have a slicer, just do what I do. It's called the "poor man's meat slicer"—a very sharp knife and a steady hand.

CHICKEN MARINADE

2 tablespoons water
1 tablespoon vegetable oil
2 teaspoons ketchup
1/2 teaspoon sugar
1/2 teaspoon salt

1/4 teaspoon paprika
1/8 teaspoon onion powder
1/8 teaspoon coarse black pepper
1/8 teaspoon savory
dash garlic powder

2 chicken breast fillets
butter-flavored spray or spread
4 whole wheat hamburger buns

2 tablespoons light mayonnaise
1 medium tomato, sliced
1 cup shredded lettuce

1. First make the marinade for the chicken breasts. In a small bowl, combine all of the ingredients for the marinade and stir well. Add the chicken breasts to the bowl and cover. Marinate the chicken for several hours. Overnight is even better.
2. When you are ready to make the sandwiches, preheat the oven to 400 degrees. Prepare to roast the chicken breasts by removing them from the marinade and placing them in a foil-lined baking pan. Bake for 20 to 25 minutes or until the chicken is fully cooked. When the chicken is cool enough to handle, slice each breast very thinly with a sharp knife. If you have a meat slicer, that works even better.
3. Preheat a frying pan or griddle to medium heat. Apply butter-flavored spread or spray to the faces of the top and bottom wheat buns. Grill the bun faces lightly on the hot cooking surface until light brown.
4. Build each sandwich by first placing one-quarter of the sliced chicken on the bottom bun.
5. Spread mayonnaise on the face of the top bun.
6. Invert the top bun. On the bun, stack a tomato slice or two, then ¼ cup of lettuce on top of that.
7. Slap the top portion of the sandwich onto the bottom and serve while the chicken is still warm. Repeat the process to make the remaining sandwiches.

- MAKES 4 SANDWICHES.

Nutrition Facts
SERVING SIZE—1 SANDWICH   FAT (PER SERVING)—6.5G
TOTAL SERVINGS—4   CALORIES (PER SERVING)—201

• • • •

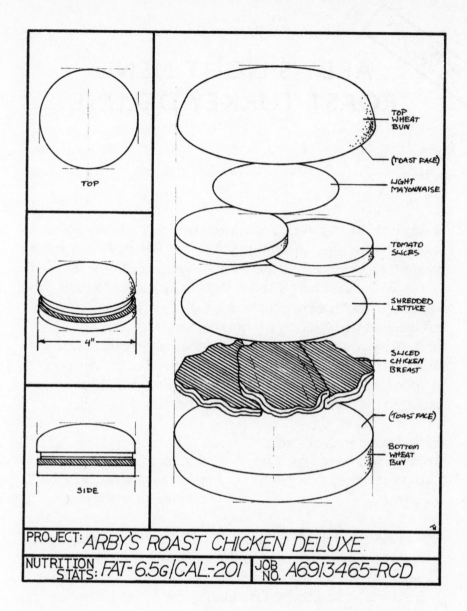

TOP

SIDE

4"

TOP
WHEAT
BUN

(TOAST FACE)

LIGHT
MAYONNAISE

TOMATO
SLICES

SHREDDED
LETTUCE

SLICED
CHICKEN
BREAST

(TOAST FACE)

BOTTOM
WHEAT
BUN

PROJECT: *ARBY'S ROAST CHICKEN DELUXE*

NUTRITION STATS: *FAT-6.5G/CAL-201*   JOB NO. *A6913465-RCD*

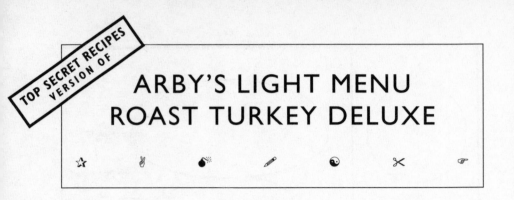

ARBY'S LIGHT MENU ROAST TURKEY DELUXE

It was in 1991 that Arby's saw a market for a selection of sandwiches that weighed in with very little fat. The chain was able to create three sandwiches that had 10 grams of fat or less, with whole wheat hamburger buns, light mayonnaise, lettuce, and tomato. Of the three selections, it is the Roast Turkey Deluxe that has the least fat, with only 6 grams per sandwich.

Now you can make a clone of that light creation, with deli-sliced roast turkey breast that you can pick up at any deli counter at your local supermarket. You can also find the turkey in prepackaged portions near the luncheon meats.

butter-flavored spray or spread
1 whole wheat hamburger bun
2 ounces deli-sliced roast turkey
  breast

salt
½ tablespoon light mayonnaise
1 to 2 tomato slices
¼ cup shredded lettuce

1. Preheat a frying pan or griddle to medium heat. Apply butter-flavored spread or spray to the faces of the top and bottom wheat buns. Grill the faces of the buns lightly on the hot pan.
2. Build the sandwich by first placing the sliced turkey on the bottom bun. Salt the turkey.
3. Spread the mayonnaise on the face of the top bun.
4. Invert the top bun. On the bun, stack the tomatoes, then the lettuce on top of that.
5. Turn the top of the sandwich over onto the bottom and serve.

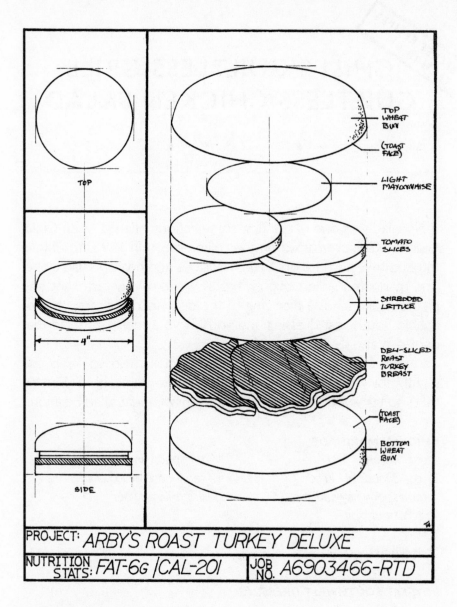

PROJECT: *ARBY'S ROAST TURKEY DELUXE*

NUTRITION STATS: *FAT-6G /CAL-201*

JOB NO. *A6903466-RTD*

- MAKES 1 SANDWICH.

Nutrition Facts

SERVING SIZE—1 SANDWICH
TOTAL SERVINGS—1

FAT (PER SERVING)—6G
CALORIES (PER SERVING)—201

• • • •

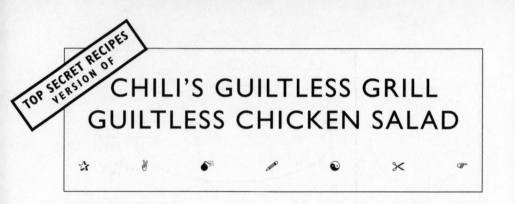

CHILI'S GUILTLESS GRILL
GUILTLESS CHICKEN SALAD

☆   ✌   💣   ✏   ☯   ✂   ☞

This salad was one of the first six selections offered when Chili's Guiltless Grill premiered on the chain's menu in 1993. You'll love the Southwestern flavors in this delicious and healthy salad clone. The marinated grilled chicken has a sweet, smoky taste, and the pico de gallo lends a nice zing to the dish. Top it all off with irresistible Southwest dressing and you'll have a meal-size salad that comes in at only 5 grams of fat.

Fat-free sour cream and low-fat milk help to keep the slightly spicy dressing remarkably low in fat grams. It's a dressing that's so tasty you'll want to use it for other low-fat salad creations.

CHICKEN MARINADE

1 cup water
1/4 cup pineapple juice
1 tablespoon soy sauce
1/2 teaspoon salt

1/4 teaspoon liquid smoke
1/4 teaspoon onion powder
dash garlic powder

2 chicken breast fillets

LOW-FAT SOUTHWEST DRESSING

1/4 cup low-fat milk
1 tablespoon vinegar
2 tablespoons minced tomato
1 tablespoon minced white onion
2 teaspoons minced canned
    ortega chili
1 teaspoon sugar

1/4 teaspoon salt
1/8 teaspoon chili powder
1/8 teaspoon cumin
dash thyme
dash oregano
1/2 cup fat-free sour cream

PICO DE GALLO

1 large tomato
¼ cup diced Spanish onion
1 teaspoon chopped fresh
   jalapeño pepper, seeded

1 teaspoon finely minced fresh
   cilantro
pinch of salt

4 cups chopped iceberg lettuce
4 cups chopped green leaf lettuce
1 cup shredded red cabbage
¼ cup shredded carrot
2 cups alfalfa sprouts

⅔ cup canned dark red kidney
   beans
2 green onions, diced
   (green part only)

1. Make the chicken marinade by combining the ingredients in a medium bowl. Add the chicken fillets and marinate for at least 24 hours.
2. Prepare the dressing by combining all ingredients, except the sour cream, in a blender. Blend on low speed for about 15 seconds or until the onion is pulverized.
3. Pour the mixture into a medium bowl and add the sour cream. Whisk until smooth. Cover and chill.
4. Prepare the pico de gallo by combining all of the ingredients in a small bowl. Cover and chill.
5. When you are ready to build the salads, cook the chicken fillets on a preheated barbecue or indoor grill set to high for 4 to 7 minutes per side, or until done.
6. To build the salad, first toss the lettuces, cabbage, and shredded carrot together. Divide this lettuce mixture and arrange it on two plates.
7. Divide the sprouts and sprinkle them over the lettuce around the edge of each plate.
8. Divide the kidney beans and sprinkle them over the lettuce on each plate.
9. Divide the pico de gallo and sprinkle it over the top of the salads.
10. Divide the green onion and sprinkle it over the top of each salad.
11. Slice the chicken fillets into bite-size pieces and arrange

over the top of each salad. Serve with the low-fat dressing on the side.

- MAKES 2 LARGE ENTRÉE SALADS.

Nutrition Facts

SERVING SIZE—1 SALAD FAT (PER SERVING)—5G
TOTAL SERVINGS—2 CALORIES (PER SERVING)—558

• • • •

CHILI'S GUILTLESS GRILL GUILTLESS CHICKEN SANDWICH

Here's another item that has been on Chili's Guiltless Grill menu from the start. It's a chicken sandwich that gets its sweet smoky flavor from the marinated chicken that is grilled over an open flame. The chicken is stacked on whole wheat buns with lettuce and tomato; and a tasty, yet simple-to-make honey mustard sauce is drizzled over the top. If your chicken fillets are too plump, just give 'em a few whacks with a tenderizing mallet and rejoice in the extra calories you work off.

MARINADE

1 cup water
1/4 cup pineapple juice
1 tablespoon soy sauce
1/2 teaspoon salt

1/4 teaspoon liquid smoke
1/4 teaspoon onion powder
dash garlic powder

4 chicken breast fillets

FAT-FREE HONEY MUSTARD DRESSING

2 tablespoons Grey Poupon Dijon
   mustard
2 tablespoons honey

1 tablespoon fat-free mayonnaise
1 teaspoon vinegar

4 whole wheat hamburger buns
1 cup shredded lettuce

4 large tomato slices

1. Prepare the chicken marinade by combining the marinade ingredients in a medium bowl. Add the chicken fillets, cover, and refrigerate for several hours. Overnight is even better.
2. When the chicken has marinated, cook the fillets on a preheated barbecue or indoor grill set to a high temperature for 4 to 7 minutes per side or until done.
3. While the chicken is grilling, make the fat-free dressing by mixing together the dressing ingredients in a small bowl.
4. Build each sandwich by first stacking one-quarter of the lettuce on the bottom hamburger bun.
5. Stack the tomato slice on the lettuce.
6. Stack the chicken fillet on the tomato.
7. Cover each sandwich with the top bun and serve with the fat-free honey mustard dressing on the side.

- SERVES 4.

Nutrition Facts

SERVING SIZE—1 SANDWICH	FAT (PER SERVING)—8G
TOTAL SERVINGS—4	CALORIES (PER SERVING)—378

• • • •

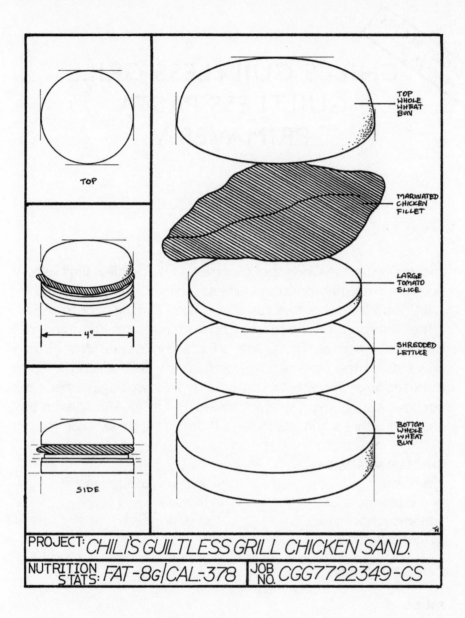

TOP

TOP
WHOLE
WHEAT
BUN

MARINATED
CHICKEN
FILLET

LARGE
TOMATO
SLICE

4"

SHREDDED
LETTUCE

BOTTOM
WHOLE
WHEAT
BUN

SIDE

PROJECT: *CHILI'S GUILTLESS GRILL CHICKEN SAND.*

NUTRITION STATS: *FAT-8g/CAL.-378*

JOB NO. *CGG7722349-CS*

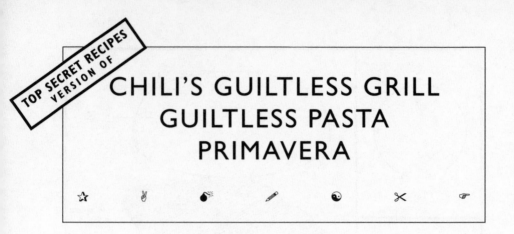

CHILI'S GUILTLESS GRILL GUILTLESS PASTA PRIMAVERA

According to one Chili's spokesperson, "The Guiltless Grill selections are extremely popular. Guiltless Grill was a smash from the start." And to ensure that customers keep coming back to these lighter selections on the menu, Chili's often rotates items and introduces new ones. The Guiltless Pasta Primavera is one of the new kids on the block among the Guiltless Grill selections. This clone recipe of the recent favorite dish makes two huge dinner-size portions, just like the restaurant serves. The recipe should even be enough for three, perhaps four—if there's a big dessert coming.

CHICKEN MARINADE

1 cup water
1/4 cup pineapple juice
1 tablespoon soy sauce
1/2 teaspoon salt

1/4 teaspoon liquid smoke
1/4 teaspoon onion powder
dash garlic powder

2 chicken breast fillets

SAUCE

2 15-ounce cans tomato sauce
1 1/2 cups water
1/2 cup diced onion
2 cloves garlic, minced
1 tomato, diced
1 tablespoon dried parsley
1 tablespoon brown sugar

2 teaspoons lemon juice
2 teaspoons red wine vinegar
1 teaspoon dried basil
1 teaspoon dried oregano
1/2 teaspoon salt
1/4 teaspoon pepper

1 1-pound package penne pasta
4 quarts water
1 summer squash, sliced
1 zucchini, sliced
1 slice red onion, halved and
    separated

¼ red bell pepper, seeded and
    sliced
¼ green bell pepper, seeded and
    sliced
salt
pepper

1. Prepare the chicken marinade by combining the marinade ingredients in a medium bowl. Add the chicken breast fillets to
   the marinade, cover, and refrigerate for 24 hours. If you're in a
   hurry, you can get by with a minimum of four hours' marinating
   time, although the flavors will not be as intense.
2. When the chicken is marinated, prepare the sauce by combining all of the ingredients in a large saucepan over high heat.
   Bring the sauce to a boil, then reduce the heat to low and
   simmer for 1 to 1½ hours or until the diced tomato is soft,
   the onions are translucent, and the sauce thickens.
3. About 20 minutes before the sauce is done, prepare the
   penne pasta by bringing 4 quarts of water to a boil. Dump the
   penne into the water, stir, and cook for 11 to 15 minutes or
   until it is *al dente*, or tender but not soft. Drain.
4. As the pasta cooks, grill the chicken fillets on a preheated barbecue or indoor grill set to a high temperature for 4 to 7 minutes per side or until done.
5. As the pasta and chicken cook, steam the vegetables in a steam
   basket over boiling water or in a steamer, for 8 to 10 minutes
   or until tender. Salt and pepper the vegetables to taste.
6. Build the dish by arranging half of the pasta on a plate. Distribute half of the vegetables over the pasta and spoon the
   marinara sauce over the top. Slice a chicken fillet into bite-size
   pieces and arrange over the top of the pasta. Repeat for the
   second serving.

• MAKES 2 LARGE DINNER-SIZE PORTIONS.

Nutrition Facts

SERVING SIZE—
   1 DINNER-SIZE PORTION
TOTAL SERVINGS—2

FAT (PER SERVING)—15G
CALORIES (PER SERVING)—1200

• • • •

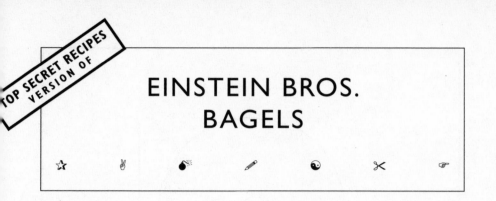

EINSTEIN BROS.
BAGELS

According to legend, in 1683 a Jewish baker shaped dough into the form of a riding stirrup to honor King John Sobieski of Poland, a skilled horseman who had saved the Austrian people from Turkish invaders. Three hundred years later, this Boulder, Colorado, chain is the biggest seller of what has become America's favorite low-fat munchies. Since the first Einstein Bros. Bagel store opened in 1995, the chain has quickly expanded into 38 states. Today there are around 450 Einstein Bros. Bagel stores serving 16 varieties of the chewy bread snack. The company also owns Noah's bagels, giving them another 140 stores. Each company has its own style of bagel, but both brands often win awards in local bagel contests. The company strives to open a new Einstein Bros. or Noah's somewhere in the country each business day.

Here are clones for six of the chain's most popular bagels. You'll notice that the special ingredient that sets these bagels apart from others is molasses. It's an ingredient that adds a unique sweetness and slightly dark color to these tasty, soft bagels. Check out pages 153 to 156 for fat-free flavored cream cheese recipes.

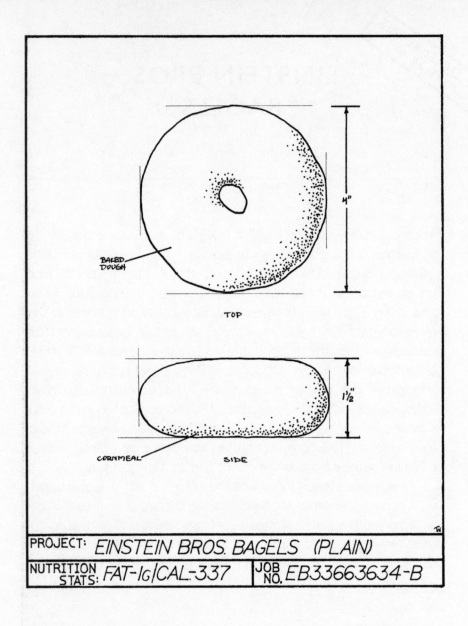

BAKED DOUGH

4"

TOP

1½"

CORNMEAL

SIDE

PROJECT: *EINSTEIN BROS. BAGELS (PLAIN)*

NUTRITION STATS: *FAT-1G/CAL.-337*   JOB NO. *EB33663634-B*

PLAIN

1 cup very warm water
  (110 to 115 degrees,
   not steaming)
½ tablespoon yeast
1 tablespoon plus 1 teaspoon
  light corn syrup
1 tablespoon plus 1 teaspoon
  molasses

½ teaspoon vegetable oil
1 teaspoon salt
2 cups bread flour (plus about
  ⅔ cup to incorporate while
  kneading)
1½ tablespoons sugar
  (for water bath)
cornmeal (for dusting)

1. Combine the warm water and yeast in a medium bowl and stir until the yeast is dissolved. Be sure the water is not too hot, or it may kill the yeast.
2. Add the corn syrup, molasses, and oil to the bowl and stir thoroughly. Add the salt.
3. Pour the 2 cups of bread flour into the bowl and incorporate it with the other ingredients.
4. Sprinkle a little of the reserved flour over the dough in the bowl and turn it out onto a surface that has been dusted with more of the reserved flour. Knead the dough, while working in the remaining reserve flour (depending on your climate you may not have to use all of the reserve flour, but you will surely use most of it). The dough should become very smooth and elastic, dry to the touch, and not tacky. You will have to knead for 6 or 7 minutes to get the right consistency.
5. Put the dough back into the bowl or another container, cover, and let it rise in a warm place for 30 to 40 minutes. The dough should double in size.
6. Punch down the dough and cut it into 4 even portions. Working with one portion of the dough at a time, form the dough into a ball. Turn the edge of the dough inward with your fingers while punching a hole in the center with your thumbs. Work the dough in a circle while stretching it out and enlarging the center hole, so that it looks like a doughnut. The hole should be between 1 to 1½ inches in diameter. Place the 4 portions of shaped dough onto a greased board or baking sheet, cover (a clean towel works well), and allow

the dough to rise for 20 to 30 minutes. The dough should nearly double in size.

7. Preheat the oven to 400 degrees.
8. Fill a medium saucepan ⅔ full of water and bring it to a boil. Add 1½ tablespoons of sugar to the water.
9. Working with one bagel at a time, first enlarge the hole if it has closed up to less than ¾ of an inch. Be careful not to overwork the dough at this point or it won't have the proper consistency. Drop the bagel into the water, cover the saucepan, and boil for 20 seconds. Flip the bagel over, and boil for another 20 seconds. Immediately take the bagel out of the water with a slotted spoon, let the water drip off for about 10 seconds, then place the bagel onto a baking sheet that has been dusted with cornmeal. Repeat for the remaining bagels. Be sure the bagels do not touch each other.
10. Bake the bagels for 26 to 30 minutes, or until they are light brown.

- MAKES 4 BAGELS.

Nutrition Facts

SERVING SIZE—1 BAGEL	FAT (PER SERVING)—1 G
TOTAL SERVINGS—4	CALORIES (PER SERVING)—337

CINNAMON SUGAR

1 cup very warm water
   (110 to 115 degrees,
   not steaming)
½ tablespoon yeast
1 tablespoon plus 1 teaspoon
   light corn syrup
1 tablespoon plus 1 teaspoon
   molasses
½ teaspoon vegetable oil

1 teaspoon salt
2 cups bread flour (plus about
   ⅔ cup to incorporate while
   kneading)
1½ tablespoons sugar
   (for water bath)
2 tablespoons superfine sugar
1½ teaspoons cinnamon
nonstick spray

1. Follow steps 1 to 8 for the plain bagels.
2. Combine superfine sugar and cinnamon in a small bowl (or use a premixed cinnamon/sugar, such as the one made by Schilling). If you have an empty shaker bottle—an empty spice bottle works well—you can put the cinnamon and sugar in it and use it to sprinkle an even coating on the bagel when the time comes.
3. Working with one bagel at a time, first enlarge the hole if it has closed up to less than ¾ of an inch. Be careful not to overwork the dough at this point or it won't have the proper consistency. Drop the bagel into the water, cover the saucepan, and boil for 20 seconds. Flip the bagel over, and boil for another 20 seconds. Immediately take the bagel out of the water with a slotted spoon, let the water drip off for about 10 seconds, sprinkle a light coating of the cinnamon/sugar over the entire surface of the bagel, then place the bagel onto a lightly greased baking sheet. Repeat for the remaining bagels. Be sure the bagels do not touch each other.
4. Bake the bagels for 26 to 30 minutes, or until they are light brown.

- MAKES 4 BAGELS.

Nutrition Facts

SERVING SIZE—1 BAGEL	FAT (PER SERVING)—1 G
TOTAL SERVINGS—4	CALORIES (PER SERVING)—360

JALAPEÑO

⅓ cup canned jalapeño slices (nacho slices)
⅛ teaspoon red pepper flakes
1 cup very warm water (110 to 115 degrees, not steaming)
½ tablespoon yeast
1 tablespoon plus 1 teaspoon light corn syrup
1 tablespoon plus 1 teaspoon molasses

½ teaspoon vegetable oil
1 teaspoon salt
2 cups bread flour (plus about ⅔ cup to incorporate while kneading)
1½ tablespoons sugar (for water bath)
cornmeal (for dusting)

1. Finely mince the jalapeño slices, then combine with the red pepper flakes in a small bowl and set aside.
2. Follow all of the steps for the plain bagels, adding the jalapeño mixture to the dough in step 2.
3. Rise and bake using the same steps as for the plain bagels.

- MAKES 4 BAGELS.

Nutrition Facts
SERVING SIZE—1 BAGEL

TOTAL SERVINGS—4

FAT (PER SERVING)—1G

CALORIES (PER SERVING)—340

CHOPPED GARLIC

1 cup very warm water
(110 to 115 degrees,
not steaming)
½ tablespoon yeast
1 tablespoon plus 1 teaspoon
light corn syrup
1 tablespoon plus 1 teaspoon
molasses
2 teaspoons vegetable oil

1 teaspoon salt
2 cups bread flour (plus about
⅔ cup to incorporate while
kneading)
1½ tablespoons sugar
(for water bath)
cornmeal (for dusting)
1 tablespoon dry minced garlic
1 teaspoon sesame seeds

1. Follow the same steps as for the plain bagels through step 9. After the bagels have been arranged on the cornmeal-dusted baking sheet, and while they are still moist, sprinkle a scant teaspoon of dry minced garlic over the top of each one. Sprinkle about ¼ teaspoon of sesame seeds over the top of each bagel as well.
2. Bake the bagels for 26 to 30 minutes, or until they are light brown.

- MAKES 4 BAGELS.

Nutrition Facts
SERVING SIZE—1 BAGEL

TOTAL SERVINGS—4

FAT (PER SERVING)—3G

CALORIES (PER SERVING)—366

CHOPPED ONION

1 cup very warm water
   (110 to 115 degrees,
    not steaming)
½ tablespoon yeast
1 tablespoon plus 1 teaspoon
   light corn syrup
1 tablespoon plus 1 teaspoon
   molasses
½ teaspoon vegetable oil

1 teaspoon salt
1 teaspoon poppy seeds
2 cups bread flour (plus about
   ⅔ cup to incorporate while
   kneading)
1½ tablespoons sugar
   (for water bath)
cornmeal (for dusting)
1 tablespoon dry minced onion

1. Follow the directions for the plain bagels through step 9, but add the poppy seeds to the mixture in step 2.
2. After the bagels have been arranged on the cornmeal-dusted baking sheet, and while they are still moist, sprinkle a scant teaspoon of dry minced onion over the top of each one.
3. Bake the bagels for 26 to 30 minutes, or until they are light brown.

- MAKES 4 BAGELS.

Nutrition Facts

SERVING SIZE—1 BAGEL
TOTAL SERVINGS—4

FAT (PER SERVING)—1 G
CALORIES (PER SERVING)—340

EVERYTHING

1 cup very warm water (110 to
   115 degrees, not steaming)
½ tablespoon yeast
1 tablespoon plus 1 teaspoon
   light corn syrup
1 tablespoon plus 1 teaspoon
   molasses
1 teaspoon vegetable oil
1 teaspoon salt
2 cups bread flour (plus about
   ⅔ cup to incorporate
   while kneading)

1½ tablespoons sugar
   (for water bath)
cornmeal (for dusting)
1 tablespoon dry minced
   onion
1 tablespoon dry minced
   garlic
½ teaspoon poppy seeds
½ teaspoon caraway seeds
½ teaspoon sesame seeds
½ teaspoon kosher salt

1. Follow the directions for the plain bagels through step 9.
2. After the bagels have been arranged on the cornmeal-dusted baking sheet, and while they are still moist, sprinkle a scant teaspoon each of dry minced onion and dry minced garlic over the top of each bagel. Combine the poppy seeds, caraway seeds, sesame seeds, and kosher salt in a small bowl. Sprinkle ¼ of the mixture over the top of each bagel.
3. Bake the bagels for 26 to 30 minutes, or until they are golden brown.

• MAKES 4 BAGELS.

Nutrition Facts

SERVING SIZE—1 BAGEL	FAT (PER SERVING)—2G
TOTAL SERVINGS—4	CALORIES (PER SERVING)—356

• • • •

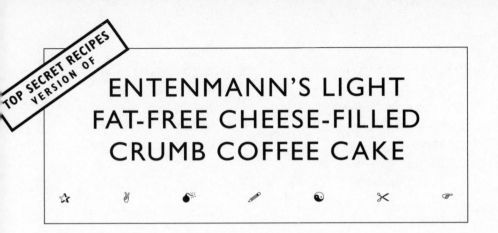

ENTENMANN'S LIGHT FAT-FREE CHEESE-FILLED CRUMB COFFEE CAKE

Take a close look at the Entenmann's logo sometime. You'll see a drawing of the same type of horse-drawn delivery wagon that William Entenmann drove back in 1898 in Brooklyn, New York, when he started his home-delivery baking service. The successful family business was passed on through the generations with little change in philosophy or goals. Then in 1951, the family realized the best way to reach the growing numbers of customers was by selling the products in New York-area supermarkets. The delivery business went retail, but the company was still a local New York-area business.

All that changed in 1982, when General Foods purchased the company. Not only did distribution go national, but at the same time food scientists at General Foods were working hard to develop the first line of fresh-baked fat-free cakes and pastries. When those products hit store shelves in 1989, the fat-shunning fad was in its infancy, and Entenmann's was able to grab a big chunk of the market.

Now you can sink your teeth into a big chunk of this home-made version of the popular cheese-filled crumb cake. This clone recipe of the popular treat makes two cakes the same size as the original, by dividing a standard 9 x 13-inch pan in half with a large piece of aluminum foil.

CAKE

½ cup Duncan Hines yellow
    cake mix
2½ cups cake flour (unsifted)
3 tablespoons Butter Buds
    Sprinkles
1 package rapid-rise yeast
    (2¼ teaspoons)

¾ teaspoon baking soda
½ teaspoon salt
1¼ cups fat-free milk
¾ teaspoon vanilla
1 tablespoon white vinegar

FILLING

2 8-ounce packages fat-free
    cream cheese
⅓ cup powdered sugar
1 tablespoon cornstarch

1 teaspoon Butter Buds Sprinkles
½ teaspoon white vinegar
½ teaspoon vanilla
¼ teaspoon salt

TOPPING

1 tablespoon yellow cake mix
¼ cup plus 1 tablespoon sugar
¼ cup all-purpose flour
2 teaspoons Butter Buds Sprinkles

½ teaspoon baking powder
dash salt
2 to 3 tablespoons fat-free ricotta
    cheese

GLAZE

1 cup powdered sugar
½ teaspoon vanilla (clear is best)
1 tablespoon plus 1 teaspoon
    fat-free milk

¼ teaspoon Butter Buds Sprinkles
pinch of salt

1. Preheat the oven to 350 degrees.
2. To make the cake, in a large bowl, combine the cake mix, cake flour, Butter Buds, yeast, baking soda, and salt.
3. In a separate, smaller bowl, combine the milk, vanilla, and vinegar, then microwave on high heat for 1½ to 2 minutes until very warm. Add the wet ingredients to the dry and beat until the mixture is well combined. Cover the bowl and set it in a warm place to rise for 10 minutes.
4. While the cake batter rises, make a custom cake pan using a 16- to 18-inch piece of foil and a 9 x 13-inch baking pan. Fold the foil in half lengthwise, then bend it up again about 1 inch to

the left and right of the middle fold. Place this foil down into the pan. This will make a liner for the baking pan with a foil divider down the middle. Spray the foil with nonstick cooking spray.

5. Pour 1 cup of the batter into each side of the pan. Bake for 5 minutes, then remove it from the oven and cool for 15 minutes.

6. As the cake cools, prepare the filling by first warming the cream cheese in the microwave on 50 percent power for 3 minutes. Add the remaining filling ingredients and beat with an electric mixer until smooth.

7. Prepare the crumb topping by combining all of the topping ingredients, except the cheese, in a small bowl. Cut the fat-free ricotta into the mixture with a knife or pastry blender until it makes crumbs about one-half to one-quarter the size of a pea.

8. Divide the cheese filling and spread half onto the top of each cake. Cover the filling with the remaining batter. Sprinkle the crumb topping over the top of the batter. Bake for 25 to 30 minutes, or until the cake begins to brown. Remove the pan from the oven and allow the cake to cool completely.

9. Make the glaze by combining the glaze ingredients in a small bowl. When the cake is cool, drizzle the glaze over the top. Store uncovered for the first day.

• MAKES 2 CRUMB CAKES.

TIDBITS

It is important to eat these cakes shortly after adding the glaze. Once the cakes are stored in a sealed container, moisture will begin to liquefy the glaze. If you plan to keep the cakes longer than a day or two, hold off on frosting the cakes until just before you eat them.

Nutrition Facts

SERVING SIZE—2.6-OUNCE SLICE   FAT (PER SERVING)—0G
TOTAL SERVINGS—18   CALORIES (PER SERVING)—140

• • • •

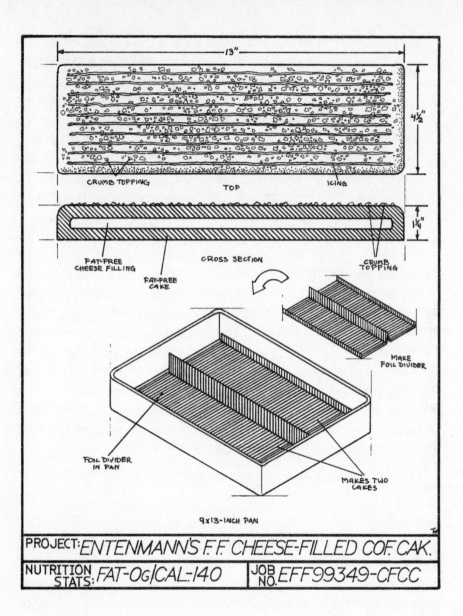

13"

4½"

CRUMB TOPPING   TOP   ICING

1¼"

FAT-FREE
CHEESE FILLING

FAT-FREE
CAKE

CROSS SECTION

CRUMB
TOPPING

MAKE
FOIL DIVIDER

FOIL DIVIDER
IN PAN

MAKES TWO
CAKES

9×13-INCH PAN

PROJECT: *ENTENMANN'S F.F. CHEESE-FILLED COF. CAK.*

NUTRITION STATS: *FAT-0G/CAL:-140*

JOB NO. *EFF99349-CFCC*

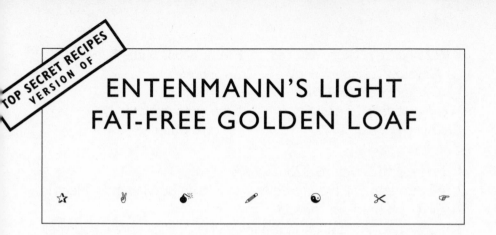

ENTENMANN'S LIGHT FAT-FREE GOLDEN LOAF

How would you like this job? Three times a day, each day, the chief bakers at Entenmann's gather in "scoring sessions," wherein they taste and rate products that come off the factory line. If a product doesn't earn at least an 8 out of 10 rating, it never makes it onto a delivery truck.

In the last ten years, Entenmann's has become known as a company that makes delicious baked fat-free products that do not taste fat-free. Today the company boasts around 50 products that carry the low-fat and fat-free labels. One of those products is a delicious pound cake, called Golden Loaf, cloned with this recipe. It makes an excellent dessert or snack when sliced and served with strawberries and low-fat whipped topping, or beneath a big scoop of light ice cream. I've also included this recipe to use with one of my favorites: the reduced-fat tiramisu found on page 197.

However you decide to serve this versatile dessert, you will amaze your guests when you tell 'em it's fat-free fare. And, yes, I realize that the reduced-fat yellow cake mix contains fat, but we have stretched out the product with cake flour so that each slice of these cakes (the recipe makes two) contains less than ½ gram. Check it out.

1 18.25-ounce package reduced-fat yellow cake mix (Betty Crocker Sweet Rewards)
¾ cup cake flour (unsifted)
1 teaspoon vanilla

2 tablespoons Butter Buds Sprinkles
½ cup sugar
1 cup egg substitute
1⅔ cups water

1. Preheat the oven to 325 degrees.
2. Mix together all the ingredients in a large bowl with an electric mixer on medium speed.
3. Spray two 9 x 5-inch loaf pans with nonstick spray. Pour half of the batter into each pan and bake for 25 minutes. Using a knife, slice down the middle of each cake (about ½-inch into the cake). This will give the cakes the same look on top as the original. Bake for an additional 20 to 25 minutes, or until the cakes are golden brown on top. Cut each cake into 13 slices.

• MAKES 2 POUND CAKES, 13 SLICES EACH.

Nutrition Facts

SERVING SIZE—1.7-OUNCE SLICE FAT (PER SERVING)—0G
TOTAL SERVINGS—26   CALORIES (PER SERVING)—106

• • • •

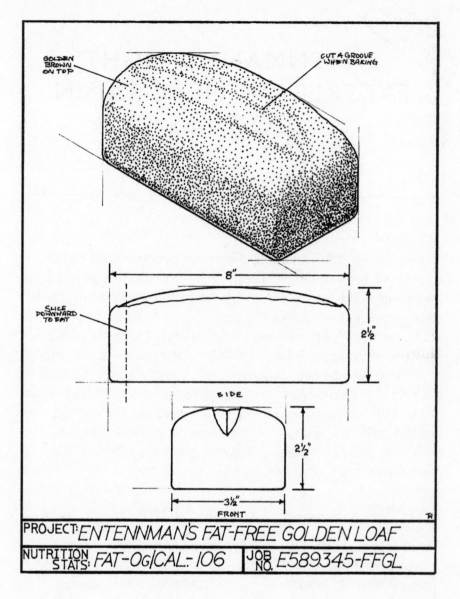

GOLDEN BROWN ON TOP

CUT A GROOVE WHEN BAKING

SLICE DOWNWARD TO EAT

8"

2½"

SIDE

2½"

3½"

FRONT

PROJECT: *ENTENNMAN'S FAT-FREE GOLDEN LOAF*

NUTRITION STATS: *FAT-0g/CAL.-106*   **JOB NO.** *E589345-FFGL*

ENTENMANN'S LIGHT FAT-FREE OATMEAL RAISIN COOKIES

These chewy little fat-free cookies have become quite popular in recent years. And they're pretty tasty considering there's a big goose egg in the fat column. A typical oatmeal cookie would have somewhere in the neighborhood of 3 grams of fat ... each. Since we're removing all the fat, we'll have to resort to some of our *Top Secret* tricks to keep these clones nice and chewy like the original.

The sweetened condensed milk, molasses, and raisin puree will certainly help by not only giving the cookies a delicious flavor, but will also create the perfect chewy texture. Sweetened condensed milk can be found in a fat-free variety that is made with skim milk, and raisin puree is easy to make in a blender. Plus, that raisin flavor is just what we want for this recipe.

2 egg whites
½ cup sugar
3 tablespoons sweetened
    condensed skim milk
1 teaspoon vanilla extract
2 tablespoons molasses
2 tablespoons raisin puree
    (see tidbit)
½ cup quick-cooking oats

¾ cup unbleached flour
¾ cup whole wheat flour
¼ cup dry nonfat milk
½ teaspoon salt
½ teaspoon baking powder
½ teaspoon baking soda
¼ teaspoon cinnamon
½ cup dark raisins

1. Preheat the oven to 325°.
2. Whip the egg whites with an electric mixer until they form soft peaks. Add the sugar, a little bit at a time, while beating.
3. Add the condensed milk, vanilla, molasses, and raisin puree and beat until well combined.
4. Use a blender or food processor to grind the oats into coarse flour. Pulse the machine a few times to pulverize the oats, but don't grind too long. You still want to see some of the oats in the cookie.
5. Combine the ground oatmeal with the remaining ingredients, except for the raisins, in another bowl and mix by hand.
6. Pour the dry mixture into the wet. Mix by hand until well combined.
7. Add the raisins to the cookie dough, and mix once again by hand.
8. Drop the dough by the tablespoonful onto a greased cookie sheet. Form the cookies into circles, and press down on them to flatten a bit.
9. Bake the cookies for 10 to 15 minutes or until they begin to turn slightly brown around the edges.

- MAKES 2 DOZEN COOKIES.

TIDBIT

Make raisin puree by combining ¼ cup raisins with ½ cup water in a blender. Blend on high speed until smooth.

Nutrition Facts

SERVING SIZE—2 COOKIES	FAT (PER SERVING)—0G
TOTAL SERVINGS—12	CALORIES (PER SERVING)—120

• • • •

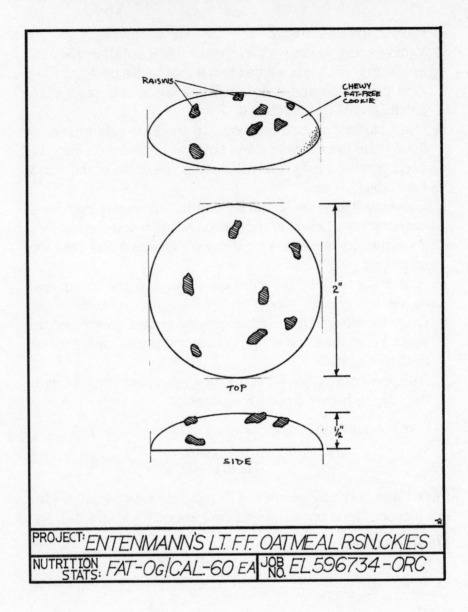

RAISINS

CHEWY
FAT-FREE
COOKIE

2"

TOP

1/2"

SIDE

PROJECT: *ENTENMANN'S LT. F.F. OATMEAL RSN. CKIES*

NUTRITION STATS: *FAT-0g/CAL.-60 EA*

JOB NO. *EL 596734-ORC*

EL POLLO LOCO
SALSA

Along with your order from this 250-unit Western U.S. chain, comes a delicious, yet simple to clone, fat-free salsa. If you don't have a food processor, never fear. You can also make the salsa by hand, with a large, sharp knife and some steady-handed, energetic, calorie-burning mincing action. Keep your head down, legs slightly spread, and watch the fingers. You don't want the salsa too red.

2 medium tomatoes, quartered
½ fresh jalapeño pepper, stem
   and seeds removed

2 leaves fresh cilantro
¼ teaspoon salt

Combine all the ingredients in a food processor. Pulse 3 to 5 times on low speed until the vegetables are well chopped. Be careful that you don't overchop and puree the ingredients. Pour everything, including the liquid, into a medium bowl. Cover and chill for several hours.

- MAKES 1 CUP.

Nutrition Facts
   SERVING SIZE—1 OUNCE
   TOTAL SERVINGS—8

FAT (PER SERVING)—0G
CALORIES (PER SERVING)—6

• • • •

GARDENBURGER ORIGINAL VEGGIE PATTY

In the early eighties, at his Gardenhouse restaurant, Chef Paul Wenner created a unique meatless patty to replace hamburgers. The patty, which contained mushrooms, brown rice, onions, oats, and low-fat cheeses, was dubbed the Gardenburger and quickly became a hit. Soon, Wenner closed his restaurant and began to concentrate on marketing his meatless, low-fat creation to a hungry, health-conscious America. Today Gardenburger patties can be found in more than 35,000 food service outlets around the world, and more than 20,000 stores.

Now you can make a surprisingly accurate clone of the real thing with the same type of ingredients Wenner uses. Most of the ingredients can be found at your local supermarket, although you may have to go to a health food store for the bulgur wheat. And if you jog over there, you can burn off what little calories you gain from this amazing kitchen clone.

2 tablespoons bulgur wheat
1 pound mushrooms, quartered
    (4 cups steamed)
1 cup diced onion (½ cup
    steamed)
½ cup rolled oats
⅔ cup cooked brown rice
½ cup shredded low-fat
    mozzarella cheese
2 tablespoons shredded low-fat
    cheddar cheese
2 tablespoons low-fat cottage
    cheese
½ teaspoon salt
½ teaspoon garlic powder
dash pepper
2 tablespoons cornstarch
olive oil cooking spray

1. Add ¼ cup boiling water to the bulgur wheat in a small bowl and let it sit for about 60 minutes. The wheat will swell to about double in size.
2. Steam the quartered mushrooms for 10 minutes or until tender, then remove them from your steamer, and replace with the onion. Steam the diced onion for 10 minutes or until the pieces are translucent. Keep these two ingredients separate, and set aside.
3. Add ½ cup of water to the oats and let them soak for about 10 minutes, until soft.
4. Drain any excess water from the bulgur wheat and oats, then combine the grains with the steamed mushrooms, rice, cheeses, and spices in a food processor and pulse 4 or 5 times until ingredients are chopped fine, but not pureed. You want a coarse texture with some identifiable chunks of grain, mushroom, and cheese.
5. Pour the mixture into a bowl with the steamed onion and cornstarch, and mix well.
6. Preheat the oven to 300 degrees and set a large skillet over medium/low heat.
7. Spray the skillet with a light coating of olive oil cooking spray. Measure ½ cup at a time of the patty mixture into the pan and shape with a spoon into a 3¾-inch patty that is approximately ½-inch thick. Cook the patties in batches for 2 to 4 minutes per side, or until light brown on the surface.
8. When all of the patties have been cooked in the skillet, arrange them on a lightly sprayed baking sheet and bake for 20 to 25 minutes in the oven. Be sure to turn them over halfway through the cooking time. You can serve the patties immediately, or freeze them, like the original, when they have cooled.
9. If you freeze the patties, you can reheat them several ways. Simply spray a light coating of olive oil cooking spray on each side and heat each patty in a pan over medium heat for 3 to 4 minutes per side until it is hot in the center. You can also use a grill to prepare the patties. Just be sure to spray each frozen patty with the oil, and be sure the flames are low. Cook for 3 to 4 minutes per side. Those are the best cooking methods;

however, you can also prepare a frozen patty by microwaving it for 30 to 35 seconds, then turning the patty over and zapping it for another 30 to 35 seconds. Finally, you can heat a frozen patty in the microwave for 30 to 35 seconds, then place the partially defrosted patty in a toaster or toaster oven and cook it on medium heat until it's hot in the center.

- MAKES 6 VEGGIE PATTIES.

TIDBITS

If your food processor is too small to hold all of the ingredients, simply divide the ingredients and process one half at a time, or cut the recipe in half. Bulgur wheat can be found in most health food stores, and even some supermarkets carry it.

Nutrition Facts

SERVING SIZE—1 PATTY   FAT (PER SERVING)—3G

TOTAL SERVINGS—6   CALORIES (PER SERVING)—135

• • • •

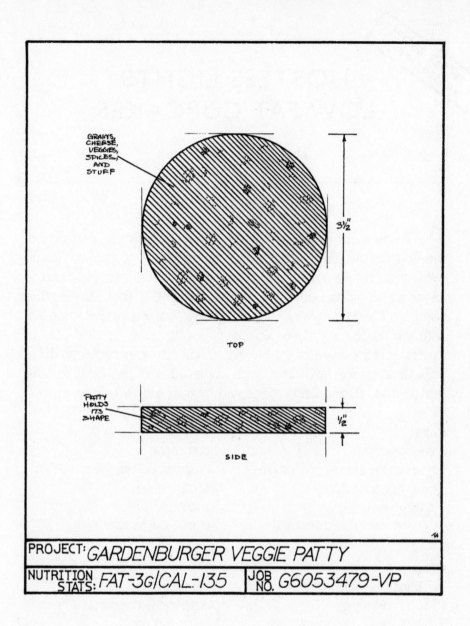

GRAINS, CHEESE, VEGGIES, SPICES, AND STUFF

3½"

TOP

PATTY HOLDS ITS SHAPE

½"

SIDE

PROJECT: *GARDENBURGER VEGGIE PATTY*	
NUTRITION STATS: *FAT-3g/CAL-135*	JOB NO. *G6053479-VP*

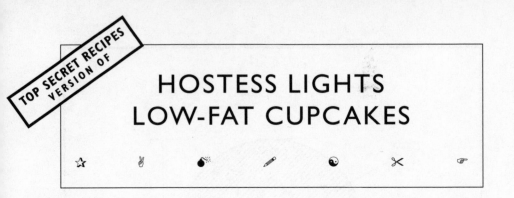

HOSTESS LIGHTS LOW-FAT CUPCAKES

The Twinkie company, otherwise known as Hostess, was one of the first to introduce reduced-fat baked goods to the masses. In 1990 the company took its most popular products and created lower-fat versions under the "Hostess Lights" label. Among the company's well-known low-fat offerings is this popular cupcake, with its trademark seven loops of white icing on the top of frosted, crème-filled cake. Here's a way you can recreate these popular cupcakes at home, with applesauce in the cake to help replace the fat, and filling made with marshmallow crème.

CAKE

1 cup sugar
1/3 cup unsweetened applesauce
1/4 cup egg substitute
1 teaspoon vanilla
1 1/4 cups cake flour (unsifted)

1/2 cup cocoa
1 teaspoon baking soda
1/2 teaspoon salt
1/2 cup buttermilk
1/2 cup whole milk

FILLING

1 7-ounce jar marshmallow crème
1/3 cup shortening
2 tablespoons powdered sugar

1/4 teaspoon salt
1 teaspoon water
1/4 teaspoon vanilla

CHOCOLATE FROSTING

I cup sugar
⅓ cup cocoa powder
¼ teaspoon salt (rounded)
⅓ cup very hot water
I teaspoon vanilla

I teaspoon dark brown food
    paste coloring (optional)
I ¼ to I ½ cups powdered sugar,
    sifted

WHITE FROSTING

⅓ cup powdered sugar, sifted
I teaspoon fat-free milk

I teaspoon meringue powder
    (optional)

1. Preheat the oven to 350 degrees.
2. To make the cake, beat together the sugar, applesauce, egg substitute, and vanilla in a large bowl for one minute.
3. In a separate medium bowl combine the cake flour, cocoa, baking soda, and salt and use a wire whisk to break up any lumps of cocoa.
4. Add the dry ingredients to the previous wet ingredients and mix together. Add the buttermilk and whole milk, then beat the mixture until smooth.
5. Spoon the batter into a 12-cup muffin tin, sprayed lightly with nonstick spray. Bake for 20 to 24 minutes or until a toothpick inserted into the center of the cake comes out clean. Turn the cupcakes out onto a cooling rack.
6. As the cupcakes cool, prepare the filling by combining ¼ teaspoon salt with I teaspoon water in a small bowl or cup. Microwave for 10 to 20 seconds on high, then stir until the salt is dissolved.
7. Beat the marshmallow crème with the shortening in a medium bowl with an electric mixer until smooth and fluffy. Add the powdered sugar, salt, water, and vanilla and beat well.
8. When the cakes have cooled, use a toothpick to poke a hole in the top of each cupcake. Swirl the toothpick around inside the cake to make room for the filling. Fill each cupcake with about 2 teaspoons of the filling.
9. For the chocolate frosting, measure I cup of sugar and ⅓ cup of cocoa powder into a deep I½- to 2-quart Pyrex bowl.

Add a rounded ¼ teaspoon of salt and mix the ingredients together.

10. Add the ⅓ cup of very hot water and the vanilla to the mixture and stir until all ingredients are well combined.

11. Loosely cover the bowl with plastic wrap and microwave at 50 percent power for 2 minutes. Stir carefully to continue dissolving the sugar crystals. Then replace the plastic wrap tightly over the bowl. Microwave on high in 30-second increments (to avoid boiling over) for 2 minutes. The mixture should begin to bubble, but watch it carefully so that it doesn't boil over. Remove the mixture from the microwave, poke holes in the plastic wrap so that steam will escape, and let the mixture stand for 15 minutes.

12. Carefully uncover the bowl (the contents will be very hot). Add 1 teaspoon dark brown food paste coloring to the hot syrup (this is an optional step that creates dark frosting like the original).

13. Stir in the sifted powdered sugar, ½ cup at a time. Mix thoroughly after each addition. You may need to add a few drops of water to the frosting to make it easier to spread. Spread about 2 teaspoons of frosting on each cupcake. You may want to moisten your knife to help the frosting spread on smoothly.

14. Make the white frosting for the design on the top of the cupcakes by mixing ⅓ cup sifted powdered sugar with 1 teaspoon nonfat milk. Add 1 teaspoon of meringue powder to the mixture, if you like, to make the frosting more opaque, like the original. Use a pastry bag with a #3 tip and make small loops down the middle of the top of each frosted cupcake.

• MAKES 12 CUPCAKES.

TIDBITS

You can create small pastry bags for the filling and the white frosting decoration by cutting the corner off of small plastic storage bags. First add the filling or frosting to the bag, then just clip the tip of a corner with scissors. Also, the cupcakes are best if eaten within a couple days of filling.

Nutrition Facts

Serving size— 1 cupcake   Fat (per serving)—1.5g

Total servings—12   Calories (per serving)—220

• • • •

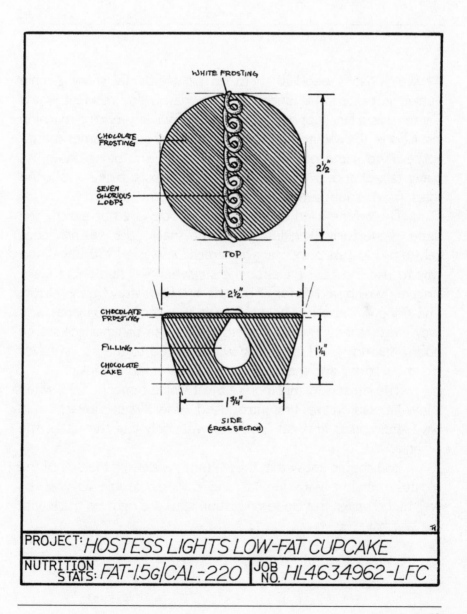

WHITE FROSTING

CHOCOLATE
FROSTING

SEVEN
GLORIOUS
LOOPS

2½"

TOP

2½"

CHOCOLATE
FROSTING

FILLING

CHOCOLATE
CAKE

1¼"

1¾"

SIDE
(CROSS SECTION)

PROJECT: *HOSTESS LIGHTS LOW-FAT CUPCAKE*

NUTRITION STATS: *FAT-1.5G/CAL-220*   JOB NO. *HL4634962-LFC*

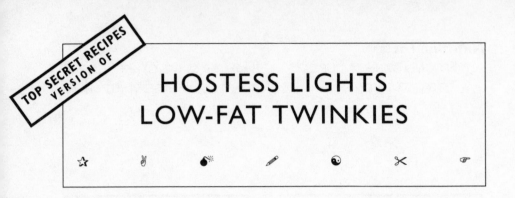

HOSTESS LIGHTS
LOW-FAT TWINKIES

Howdy Doody peddled them on his 1950s TV show. Archie Bunker got one in his lunchbox every day. Even President Jimmy Carter was a fan, supposedly ordering a Twinkie vending machine installed in the White House. Yes, Twinkies are an American favorite. And if the oblong little snack cake isn't being eaten, it's being talked about; usually by talk show hosts joking about the snack food's supposedly long shelf life.

The crème-filled cakes we know today are not exactly the same as the early Twinkies. When the snack cake was first conceived by Hostess plant manager James Dewar in 1930, it was as a way to use the cake pans for the strawberry "Little Short Cake Fingers," which sat idle for all but the six-week strawberry season. The filling in those original cakes was flavored with bananas, and they were called "Twinkle Fingers." But when bananas got scarce during World War II the filling was changed to the vanilla flavor we know today, and the name was shortened to "Twinkies."

The latest reformulation of the Twinkie came in 1990, when a low-fat version was first introduced. Now Twinkie lovers could have their cakes and eat 'em too, with only half the fat of the original.

You should know that these clones are twice the size of the Hostess version, with the fat and calories double as well. By weight, however, this clone's nutrition stats are right on track with the original.

CAKE

I cup egg substitute	2 cups unsifted cake flour
I egg white	I tablespoon baking powder
1⅔ cups sugar	½ teaspoon salt
½ teaspoon vanilla	½ cup fat-free milk
⅛ teaspoon lemon extract	1½ teaspoons vegetable oil
12 12 x 12-inch pieces of aluminum foil	nonstick cooking spray

FILLING

¼ teaspoon salt	⅓ cup shortening
2 teaspoons water	2 tablespoons powdered sugar
I 7-ounce jar marshmallow crème	¼ teaspoon vanilla

1. Preheat the oven to 325 degrees.
2. In a large glass or metal bowl (copper is best—don't use plastic), beat together the egg substitute egg white until thick and lemon-colored. Add sugar, vanilla, and lemon extract and beat until smooth.
3. In another bowl, mix together the flour, baking powder, and salt.
4. Fold the dry mixture into the wet. Don't overmix.
5. In a small microwave-safe bowl, combine the fat-free milk with the oil. Heat this mixture in the microwave on high for 1½ minutes, or until it is very hot, but not boiling.
6. Fold the hot milk mixture into the batter. Do not beat and don't overmix.
7. Prepare the cake molds by folding each square of foil in half and then in half again, so that each piece is a 6-inch square. Wrap each of these foil pieces around a spice bottle. Fold the ends and leave the side open, so that when the foil is removed it makes a small pan (see diagram on page 67). Spray the inside of each mold with nonstick cooking spray. Then, arrange the molds in one or two baking dishes so that they can't tip over when baking.
8. Fill each mold about halfway with batter. Bake the cakes for

25 to 30 minutes or until the tops of the cakes turn light brown. Remove the cakes from the oven, and when they have cooled enough to touch, peel the foil off of each one and place them flat side (the top when baking) down onto wax paper or a cooling rack.

9. As the cakes cool, prepare the filling by combining ¼ teaspoon salt with 1 teaspoon water in a small microwave-safe bowl or cup. Microwave for 10 to 20 seconds on high, then stir until the salt is dissolved.

10. Beat the marshmallow crème with the shortening in a medium bowl with an electric mixer until smooth and fluffy. Add the powdered sugar, salt, water, and vanilla and beat well.

11. When the cakes have cooled, use a toothpick to poke three holes along the flat side of the cake (the top when baking). Swirl the toothpick around inside the cake to make room for the filling.

12. Squirt crème filling into each of the three holes in each of the cakes. Be careful not to overfill the cakes or you will have a sticky explosion that must be eaten immediately.

- MAKES 12 SNACK CAKES.

TIDBITS

If you want the cake to be yellow, like the original, you will have to be selective when choosing egg substitute. Scramblers brand egg substitute seems to make the cake the deepest yellow. Or, if you don't use Scramblers, you can add a couple drops of yellow food coloring. These snack cakes are best if eaten within a couple days of filling.

Nutrition Facts

SERVING SIZE—1 SNACK CAKE   FAT (PER SERVING)—3G
TOTAL SERVINGS—12   CALORIES (PER SERVING)—280

• • • •

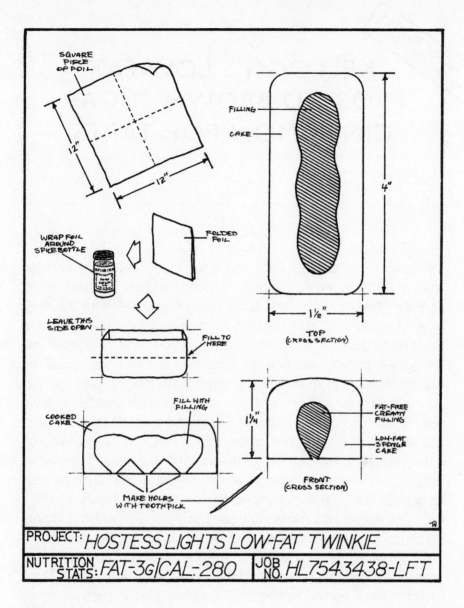

SQUARE PIECE OF FOIL

12"

12"

WRAP FOIL AROUND SPICE BOTTLE

FOLDED FOIL

LEAVE THIS SIDE OPEN

FILL TO HERE

FILLING

CAKE

4"

1½"

TOP
(CROSS SECTION)

COOKED CAKE

FILL WITH FILLING

MAKE HOLES WITH TOOTHPICK

1¼"

FAT-FREE CREAMY FILLING

LOW-FAT SPONGE CAKE

FRONT
(CROSS SECTION)

PROJECT:	HOSTESS LIGHTS LOW-FAT TWINKIE	
NUTRITION STATS:	FAT-3g/CAL-280	JOB NO. HL7543438-LFT

KELLOGG'S LOW-FAT FROSTED BROWN SUGAR CINNAMON POP-TARTS

☆　　♉　　💣　　✏　　◉　　✂　　☞

Not even Tony the Tiger is a match for the world's most beloved toaster pastries. While Kellogg's Frosted Flakes is the best-selling cereal in the U.S., Pop-Tarts are an even bigger seller for the food manufacturer, with $330 million in sales in 1996. The two-to-a-pack rectangular snacks were born in 1964, when Kellogg's followed a competitor's idea for breakfast pastries that could be heated through in an ordinary toaster. With the company's experience in cereals and grains it was able to create pastries in a variety of flavors. Pop-Tarts have always dominated the toaster pastry market, but in the first half of the 1990s Nabisco was coming on strong with its own toaster pastries called Toastettes. Toastettes became so appealing to consumers because the package held eight pastries, while Pop-Tarts still had six to a box. In June of 1996, Kellogg's added two more Pop-Tarts to each box without changing the price, and Toastettes sales quickly dropped by 45 percent.

Another move against competitor Nabisco came that same year when Kellogg's introduced its new line of low-fat Pop-Tarts. Nabisco had earlier introduced low-fat toaster pastries in its SnackWell's line, but the Kellogg's low-fat version of its popular product once again dominated.

This recipe makes eight clones, or a box's worth of the toaster pastries. Be sure to roll the dough very flat when preparing the pastries, and toast them on the very lowest setting of your toaster. Watch the pastries closely and pop 'em up if the frosting begins to turn brown.

DOUGH

2 tablespoons shortening
1/3 cup powdered sugar
3 tablespoons low fat
   (1 percent fat) buttermilk
1 tablespoon light corn syrup
1/2 teaspoon baking soda

rounded 1/4 teaspoon salt
scant 1/8 teaspoon baking powder
1 2/3 cups all-purpose flour
   (plus about 1/4 cup
   reserved for rolling dough)
3 tablespoons water

FILLING

3 tablespoons dark brown sugar
3 tablespoons sugar
3 tablespoons all-purpose flour

dash cinnamon
dash salt

1 egg white, beaten

FROSTING

1 tablespoon dark brown sugar
4 teaspoons fat-free milk
1 1/4 cups powdered sugar

dash salt
dash cinnamon

1. In a large bowl combine the shortening, powdered sugar, buttermilk, corn syrup, baking soda, salt, and baking powder using an electric mixer.
2. Add the flour and mix by hand to incorporate.
3. Mix in the water by hand, then use your hands to form the dough into a ball. Cover and set aside.
4. To make the filling, combine the ingredients in a small bowl and whisk together. Set aside.
5. To build the pastries, divide the dough in half, then roll one half out onto a floured surface, using additional flour on the rolling pin to prevent the dough from sticking. Roll the dough to no more than 1/16-inch thick. Use a knife or pizza wheel to cut the dough into four 3 x 8-inch rectangles.
6. Brush the beaten egg white over the entire surface of one half of each rectangle. Sprinkle a rounded 1/2 tablespoon of the filling over the surface of the brushed half of the pastry, being sure to leave a margin of about 1/4-inch from the edge

of the dough all of the way around. Fold the other side of the dough over onto the filling. Press down on the edge of the dough all of the way around with the tines of a fork to seal it. Use the fork to poke several holes in the top of the pastry. Fill the remaining three dough rectangles, and then repeat the process with the remaining half portion of dough.

7. Arrange the pastries on a lightly greased cookie sheet and bake in a preheated 350-degree oven 8 to 10 minutes. The pastries should be only very light brown, not dark brown (the pastries will be reheated and browned in a toaster before eating, like the real thing). Remove the pastries from the oven and cool completely.

8. Make the frosting by combining the brown sugar and milk in a small bowl. Microwave on half power for 10 to 20 seconds and stir until the sugar is dissolved. Add the remaining ingredients and stir well until smooth.

9. Spread a thin layer of the frosting over the top of each pastry and allow it to dry. Now leave the pastries out so that they dry completely. Overnight is best.

10. To reheat the pastries, toast them in a toaster oven or toaster on the lightest setting only. Watch carefully so that the pastries do not burn.

- SERVES 8.

Nutrition Facts

SERVING SIZE—1 PASTRY	FAT (PER SERVING)—3G
TOTAL SERVINGS—8	CALORIES (PER SERVING)—219

• • • •

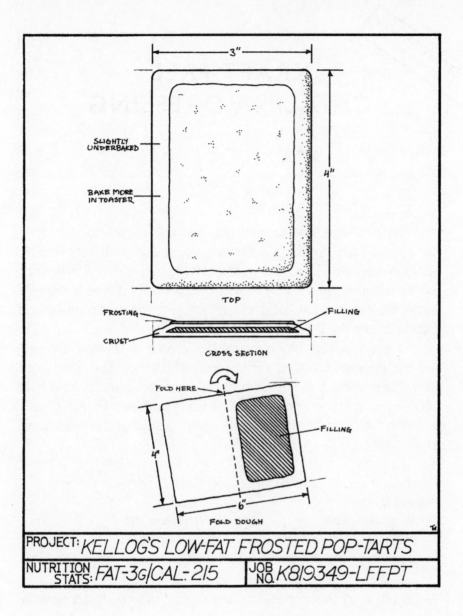

3"

SLIGHTLY
UNDERBAKED

BAKE MORE
IN TOASTER

4"

TOP

FROSTING   FILLING

CRUST

CROSS SECTION

FOLD HERE

4"

FILLING

6"

FOLD DOUGH

PROJECT: *KELLOG'S LOW-FAT FROSTED POP-TARTS*

NUTRITION STATS: *FAT-3G/CAL.-215*   JOB NO. *K819349-LFFPT*

71

KRAFT FREE
CATALINA DRESSING

In 1958, Kraft became one of the first companies to introduce low-calorie salad dressings, with dietetic versions of Italian, French, Bleu Cheese, and Thousand Island dressings. Then, in 1990, Kraft scored another series of hits with its line of fat-free dressings. Today, fat-free and low-fat dressings are just about as popular and diverse as the full-fat varieties.

Here's a TSR clone recipe to create a fat-free dressing like the popular Catalina variety from the innovative food conglomerate. Where the fat should be, cornstarch and gelatin help thicken the dressing and give it a pleasing texture that will ensure you don't even miss those big-time fat grams of the traditional stuff.

1 cup water
1/3 cup sugar
1/3 cup white vinegar
3 tablespoons tomato paste
1 teaspoon cornstarch

1/2 teaspoon Knox unflavored
   gelatin
3/4 teaspoon salt
dash garlic powder

1. Combine all the ingredients in a saucepan and stir to dissolve the gelatin and cornstarch.
2. Set the pan over medium heat until the mixture begins to boil. Boil for 1 minute, stirring often, then remove the pan from the heat, cover it, and let it cool.
3. Pour the dressing into a covered container and refrigerate it for several hours or overnight until chilled.

- Makes 1 cup.

Nutrition Facts

Serving size—2 tablespoons   Fat (per serving)—0g
Total servings—8   Calories (per serving)—40

• • • •

KRAFT FREE
CLASSIC CAESAR DRESSING

☆　✌　🔥　✏　☯　✂　☞

Thanks to fat-free mayonnaise and low-fat buttermilk, we can make a homegrown version of this popular fat-free Kraft creation. You might at first say, "Wait a minute ... how can this be fat-free when there's buttermilk and two kinds of grated cheese in there?" Yes, indeed, those products do contain fat. But, as long as a serving of the finished product contains less than ½ gram of fat—as it does here—it's considered fat-free. Be sure to give yourself plenty of time to allow this dressing to chill in the refrigerator for several hours before serving.

1 tablespoon sugar
½ teaspoon salt
2 tablespoons hot water
½ cup fat-free mayonnaise
2 tablespoons low-fat buttermilk
　　(1 percent fat)
4 teaspoons white vinegar

2 teaspoons grated Romano
　　cheese
2 teaspoons grated Parmesan
　　cheese
dash coarse ground black pepper
dash dried oregano
dash garlic powder

1. Dissolve the sugar and salt in a small bowl with the hot water. Set aside.
2. Combine the remaining ingredients in a medium bowl and stir well.
3. Add the water/sugar/salt mixture to the other ingredients and stir once more to combine. Place the dressing in a covered container in the refrigerator and chill for several hours.

- MAKES A LITTLE OVER ¾ CUP.

TIDBITS

If the dressing seems too thick, just add some more water, a table-spoon at a time, until it has the desired consistency.

Nutrition Facts

SERVING SIZE—2 TABLESPOONS   FAT (PER SERVING)—0G
TOTAL SERVINGS—7   CALORIES (PER SERVING)—35

• • • •

KRAFT FREE THOUSAND ISLAND DRESSING

☆   ✌   💣   ✏   ☯   ✂   ☞

Once upon a time we drenched our salads with generous portions of popular dressings such as this one and considered it a healthy pre-entrée course. Just two tablespoons of the full-fat version of Thousand Island dressing packs about 10 grams of fat, and we normally use about ¼ cup on a salad. That's 20 grams of fat in our bellies, before the main course has even started. Yikes! But, today we know better. So, never fear, a *Top Secret Recipe* is here. And you won't get even one gram of fat from a serving of this TSR formula that clones the most popular fat-free Thousand Island dressing on the supermarket shelves.

1 tablespoon sugar	1 tablespoon white vinegar
⅛ teaspoon salt	2 teaspoons sweet pickle relish
2 tablespoons hot water	1 teaspoon finely minced white
½ cup fat-free mayonnaise	onion
2 tablespoons ketchup	dash black pepper

1. Dissolve the sugar and salt in the hot water in a small bowl.
2. Combine the remaining ingredients with the water mixture. Stir well.
3. Place the dressing in a covered container and refrigerate it for several hours so that the flavors blend.

- MAKES ABOUT 1 CUP.

TIDBITS

If the dressing seems too thick, just add some more water, a tablespoon at a time, until it has the desired consistency.

Nutrition Facts

SERVING SIZE—2 TABLESPOONS   FAT (PER SERVING)—0G
TOTAL SERVINGS—6   CALORIES (PER SERVING)—40

• • • •

KRAFT LIGHT DELUXE MACARONI & CHEESE DINNER

The difference between the "deluxe" version of Kraft's Macaroni & Cheese Dinner and the original is the cheese. The deluxe dinner has an envelope of cheese sauce, while the original dinner, introduced to the nation back in 1937, comes with powdered cheese. The original Kraft Macaroni & Cheese Dinner is the most popular packaged dinner product around, and one of the top six best-selling of all dry goods sold in the supermarket—probably because it only takes about 7 minutes to prepare, and a box costs just 70 cents. And who doesn't like macaroni and cheese? But it's the deluxe version—the more expensive version—with its pouch of gooey, yellow cheese sauce, which Kraft reformulated as a reduced-fat product in 1997. The new version boasts 50 percent less fat and 10 percent fewer calories than the deluxe original, and tastes just as good. So here's a simple clone that requires you to get your hands on Cheez Whiz Light, reduced-fat cheddar cheese, and elbow macaroni. Then you're on your way to an amazing clone of what cartoon Texan Hank Hill from the TV show *King of the Hill* refers to as "veggies."

8 cups water
1 ¾ cups uncooked elbow macaroni
⅓ cup reduced-fat
    (2 percent milk) shredded
    cheddar cheese

½ cup Cheez Whiz Light
1 tablespoon whole milk
½ teaspoon salt

1. Bring 8 cups (2 quarts) of water to a boil over high heat in a large saucepan. Add the elbow macaroni to the water and cook for 10 to 12 minutes or until tender, stirring occasionally.
2. As the macaroni boils, prepare the sauce by combining the cheddar cheese, Cheez Whiz, and milk in a small saucepan over medium/low heat. Stir the cheese mixture often as it heats, so that it does not burn. Add the salt. When all of the cheddar cheese has melted and the sauce is smooth, cover the pan and set it aside until the macaroni has cooked.
3. When the macaroni is ready, drain the water off, but do not rinse the macaroni.
4. Using the same pan you prepared the macaroni in, combine the macaroni with the cheese sauce and mix well.

- SERVES 4.

TIDBITS

If you would like your macaroni and cheese to have a color that is similar to the happy, fluorescent orange tint of the original, you can add a little paprika—about 1/8 teaspoon—to the cheese sauce just before you remove it from the heat.

Nutrition Facts

SERVING SIZE—1 CUP	FAT (PER SERVING)—5G
TOTAL SERVINGS—4	CALORIES (PER SERVING)—290

• • • •

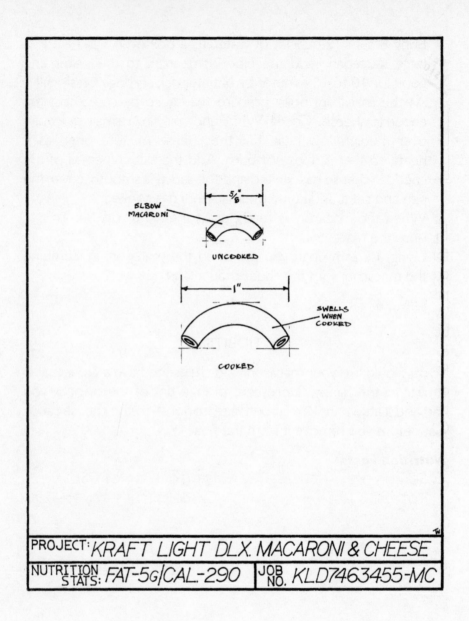

ELBOW
MACARONI

$\frac{5}{8}''$

UNCOOKED

1"

SWELLS
WHEN
COOKED

COOKED

PROJECT: *KRAFT LIGHT DLX. MACARONI & CHEESE*

NUTRITION STATS: *FAT-5G/CAL.-290*   JOB NO. *KLD7463455-MC*

NABISCO REDUCED-FAT CHEESE NIPS

In the last several years, since 1992, Nabisco has taken great effort to produce reduced-fat versions of all the popular products created by the food giant. This product loyalty–retaining move is just good business. According to one Nabisco spokesperson, "We want to bring back the people who have enjoyed our products, but went away for health and diet reasons." Indeed, that's exactly what we see happening, as customers are now grabbing for all those boxes with the green on them. The box for these cheesy crackers is indeed splashed with green and has big letters at the top that say: "Reduced Fat: 40% less fat than original Cheese Nips."

The secret ingredient for this clone of the popular little square crackers is the fat-free cheese sprinkles by Molly McButter. One 2-ounce shaker of the stuff will do it, and you won't use it all. Just keep in mind that cheese powder is pretty salty, so you may want to go very easy on salting the tops of the crackers.

1 cup sifted all-purpose flour
   (plus about 1/2 cup for
   kneading and rolling)
1 teaspoon baking soda
1/4 teaspoon baking powder

nonstick cooking spray

1/2 cup Molly McButter fat-free
   cheese sprinkles.
2 1/2 tablespoons shortening
1/3 cup plus 1 tablespoon low-fat
   buttermilk (1 percent fat)

1/2 teaspoon salt (optional for tops)

1. Sift together 1 cup of flour, the baking soda, baking powder, and cheese sprinkles in a large bowl.
2. Cut in the shortening with a fork and knife with a crosswise motion until the dough is broken down into rice-size pieces. The mixture will still be very dry.
3. Stir in the buttermilk with a fork until the dough becomes very moist and sticky.
4. Sprinkle a couple tablespoons of the reserved flour over the dough and work it in until the dough can be handled without sticking, then turn it out onto a floured board, being sure to reserve ¼ cup of flour for later. Knead the dough well for 60 to 90 seconds, and be sure the flour is incorporated. Wrap the dough in plastic wrap and chill for at least one hour.
5. Preheat the oven to 325 degrees. Spray a light coating of cooking spray on a baking sheet.
6. Remove the dough from the refrigerator and use the remaining reserved flour to dust a rolling surface. Roll about one-third of the dough to about ¹⁄₁₆-inch thick. Trim the edges square (a pizza slicer works great for this), then transfer the dough to the baking sheet. Use the rolling pin to transfer the dough. Simply pick up one end of the dough onto the rolling pin, and roll the dough around it. Reverse the process onto the baking sheet to transfer the dough.
7. Use a pizza slicer to cut across and down the dough, creating 1-inch square pieces. Use the blunt end of a skewer or a cut toothpick to poke a hole in the center of each piece.
8. Sprinkle a very light coating of salt over the top of the crackers (this is optional—the crackers will already be quite salty) and bake for 8 to 10 minutes. Mix the crackers around like Scrabble tiles (so those on the edge don't burn) and bake for another 3 to 5 minutes, or until some are just barely turning a light brown. Repeat the rolling and baking process with the remaining dough.

- MAKES APPROXIMATELY 300 CRACKERS.

Nutrition Facts

SERVING SIZE—31 CRACKERS   FAT (PER SERVING)—3.5G

TOTAL SERVINGS—ABOUT 10   CALORIES (PER SERVING)—105

• • • •

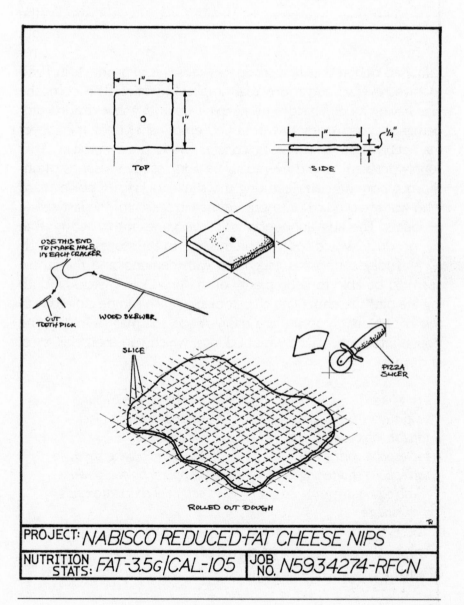

TOP

SIDE

USE THIS END
TO MAKE HOLE
IN EACH CRACKER

CUT
TOOTH PICK

WOOD SKEWER

SLICE

PIZZA
SLICER

ROLLED OUT DOUGH

PROJECT:	NABISCO REDUCED-FAT CHEESE NIPS
NUTRITION STATS:	FAT-3.5G/CAL.-105
JOB NO.	N5934274-RFCN

NABISCO SNACKWELL'S CHOCOLATE CHIP COOKIES

Nabisco debuted its first six SnackWell's line of products in 1992 to rave reviews and more than impressive sales. The company was having a very hard time keeping up with the extraordinary demand, and customers would find empty shelves in the super-markets where SnackWell's cookies were once stacked. That supply problem would eventually be addressed in a series of hu-morous commercials, featuring the shelf-stocking "Cookie Man" who was attacked by ravenous women in search of the fast-selling products. The ads' announcer told everyone not to worry, that the products would soon be on the way to the stores.

Today, supply has caught up with demand, and the stores seem to be able to keep plenty of the products in stock, includ-ing the bite-size chocolate chip cookies, which can be cloned with this recipe. The cookies are easily made so small by rolling the dough into long, plastic-wrapped logs, which you then chill, slice, and bake.

1 egg white	3/4 cup all-purpose flour
1/4 cup sugar	1/4 teaspoon plus a pinch
1 tablespoon brown sugar	of salt
1 tablespoon corn syrup	3/4 teaspoon baking soda
1 tablespoon shortening	1/2 teaspoon baking powder
1 1/2 tablespoons egg	1/2 cup mini chocolate chips
substitute	

1. Preheat the oven to 325 degrees.
2. Beat the egg white until thick.

3. Add the granulated sugar to the egg white and continue beating until the mixture forms soft peaks.
4. While beating, add the brown sugar, corn syrup, shortening, and egg substitute.
5. In a separate bowl, combine the flour, salt, baking soda, and baking powder.
6. Combine the dry mixture with the wet and mix well. Add the chocolate chips and incorporate them into the dough.
7. Divide the dough in half, then roll each portion into a long, thin log about the same diameter as a nickel and wrap each in plastic wrap. Put the dough into the refrigerator and chill it for a couple hours (you may also use the freezer for roughly half the time if you're in a hurry).
8. When the dough has thoroughly chilled, remove each log of dough from the plastic wrap and cut into ¼-inch-thick slices. Place slices on a cookie sheet coated lightly with nonstick spray about ½-inch apart, and bake for 10 to 12 minutes or until the cookies turn light brown.

• MAKES 12 DOZEN BITE-SIZE COOKIES.

Nutrition Facts

SERVING SIZE—13 COOKIES   FAT (PER SERVING)—3.3G
TOTAL SERVINGS—11   CALORIES (PER SERVING)—105

• • • •

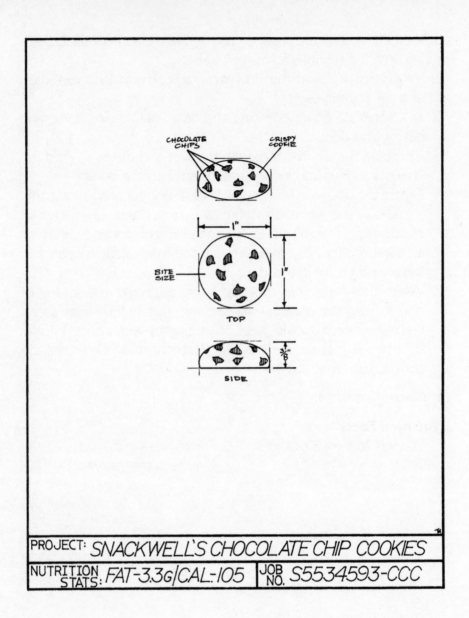

CHOCOLATE
CHIPS

CRISPY
COOKIE

1"

1"

BITE
SIZE

TOP

3/8"

SIDE

PROJECT: *SNACKWELL'S CHOCOLATE CHIP COOKIES*

NUTRITION
STATS: *FAT-3.3g/CAL.-105*

JOB
NO. *S5534593-CCC*

NABISCO SNACKWELL'S FUDGE BROWNIE BARS

One of the favorite SnackWell's creations are the very low-fat snack bars that now come in several varieties, including apple raisin, banana, golden cake, and this one, which tastes like a brownie. But, while a single brownie might contain around 6 to 10 grams of fat, this snack bar weighs in with just a fraction of that—at only 2 grams of fat per serving.

The secret to keeping the fat to a minimum in this recipe is the use of egg whites, corn syrup, and chocolate syrup. These fat-free ingredients help to replace much of the fat that would be found in a traditional recipe, while keeping the finished product moist and chewy, and filled with flavor.

2 egg whites
1 cup plus 5 tablespoons sugar
2 tablespoons corn syrup
2 tablespoons shortening
1/2 cup Hershey's chocolate syrup
1/2 cup fudge topping
1/4 cup warm water

1 teaspoon vanilla
1 1/2 cups all-purpose flour
1/4 cup cocoa
3/4 teaspoon salt
1/4 teaspoon baking soda
nonstick cooking spray

1. Preheat the oven to 350 degrees.
2. In a large bowl, whip the egg whites with an electric mixer until they become thick. Do not use a plastic bowl for this.
3. Add 1 cup of sugar to the egg whites and continue to beat until the mixture forms soft peaks.
4. To the egg white and sugar mixture, add the corn syrup, shortening, chocolate syrup, fudge, water, and vanilla.

5. In a separate bowl, combine the flour, cocoa, salt, and baking soda.
6. While beating the wet mixture, slowly add the dry mixture.
7. Lightly grease a 9 x 13-inch pan with a light coating of nonstick cooking spray. Be sure to coat the sides as well as the bottom of the pan. Dump about 3 tablespoons of the remaining sugar into the pan, then tilt and shake the pan so that a light layer of sugar coats the entire bottom of the pan and about halfway up the sides. Pour out the excess sugar.
8. Pour the batter into the pan, spreading it evenly around the inside. Sprinkle a light coating of sugar—about two tablespoons— over the entire top surface of the batter. Gently shake the pan from side to side to evenly distribute the sugar over the batter. Bake for 25 to 28 minutes or until the cake begins to pull away from the sides of the pan.
9. Remove the cake from the oven and turn it out onto a cooling rack. When the cake has cooled, place it onto a sheet of wax paper on a cutting board and slice across the cake 6 times, creating 7 even sections. Next cut the cake lengthwise twice, into thirds, creating a total of 21 snack bars. When the bars have completely cooled, store them in a resealable plastic bag or an airtight container.

• MAKES 21 SNACK BARS.

Nutrition Facts

SERVING SIZE—1 BAR   TOTAL FAT (PER SERVING)—2G
SERVINGS—21   CALORIES (PER SERVING)—144

• • • •

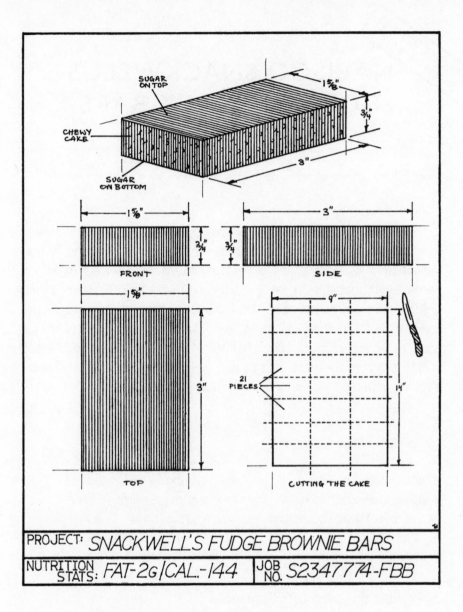

SUGAR ON TOP

CHEWY CAKE

SUGAR ON BOTTOM

1 5/8"

3/4"

3"

1 5/8"

3/4"

FRONT

3/4"

3"

SIDE

1 5/8"

3"

TOP

9"

14"

21 PIECES

CUTTING THE CAKE

PROJECT: *SNACKWELL'S FUDGE BROWNIE BARS*

NUTRITION STATS: *FAT-2g/CAL.-144*

JOB NO. *S2347774-FBB*

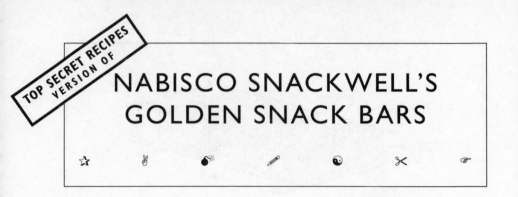

NABISCO SNACKWELL'S GOLDEN SNACK BARS

Bite into one of these chewy cake bars and you won't believe that it's so low in fat. That's because we replace a lot of the fat you would find in most cakes with sweetened condensed milk, and some egg substitute. That gives us room to throw some shortening in there and still keep the fat count at less than 2 grams per serving, just like the real thing. Also, take note of the technique used to give the snack bars that sugar-crystal coating on the top and bottom of the bars, just as you will find on the original SnackWell's creation.

2 egg whites
I cup plus 5 tablespoons
    sugar
2 tablespoons corn syrup
3 tablespoons shortening
1/4 cup sweetened condensed
    skim milk
1/4 cup egg substitute

3 tablespoons low-fat
    (2 percent) milk
1 1/2 teaspoons vanilla
1/4 teaspoon lemon extract
1 1/2 cups all-purpose flour
I teaspoon salt
1/4 teaspoon baking soda
nonstick cooking spray

1. Preheat the oven to 350 degrees.
2. In a large bowl, whip the egg whites with an electric mixer until they become thick. Do not use a plastic bowl for this.
3. Add I cup of sugar to the egg whites and continue to beat until the mixture forms soft peaks.
4. Add the corn syrup, shortening, condensed milk, egg substitute, low-fat milk, vanilla, and lemon extract to the mixture while beating.

5. In a separate bowl, combine the flour, salt, and baking soda.
6. While beating the wet mixture, slowly add the dry ingredients.
7. Lightly grease a 9 x 13-inch pan with a light coating of nonstick cooking spray. Be sure to coat the sides as well as the bottom of the pan. Dump about 3 tablespoons of sugar into the pan, then tilt and shake the pan so that a light layer of sugar coats the entire bottom of the pan and about halfway up the sides. Pour out the excess sugar.
8. Pour the batter into the pan, spreading it evenly around the inside. Sprinkle a light coating of sugar—about two tablespoons—over the entire top surface of the batter. Gently shake the pan from side to side to evenly distribute the sugar over the batter. Bake for 25 to 28 minutes or until the cake begins to pull away from the sides of the pan.
9. Remove the cake from the oven and turn it out onto a cooling rack. When the cake has cooled, place it onto a sheet of wax paper on a cutting board and slice across the cake 6 times, creating 7 even slices. Next cut the cake lengthwise twice, into thirds, creating a total of 21 snack bars. When the bars have completely cooled, store them in a resealable plastic bag or an airtight container.

• MAKES 21 SNACK BARS.

Nutrition Facts

SERVING SIZE—1 BAR	TOTAL FAT (PER SERVING)—1.8G
SERVINGS—21	CALORIES (PER SERVING)—113

• • • •

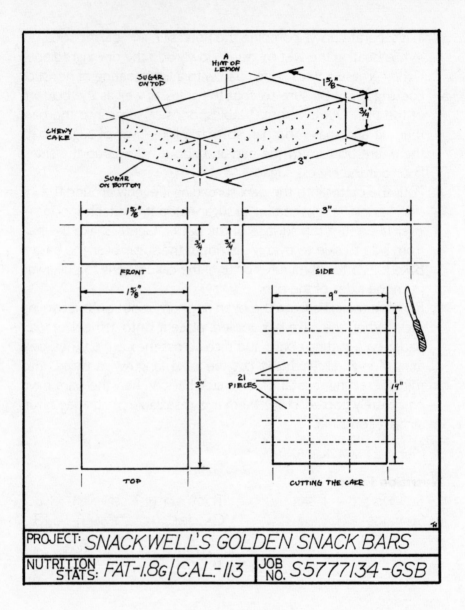

A
HINT OF
LEMON

SUGAR
ON TOP

CHEWY
CAKE

SUGAR
ON BOTTOM

1⅝"

¾"

3"

1⅝"

¾"

¾"

3"

FRONT

SIDE

1⅝"

3"

TOP

9"

21
PIECES

14"

CUTTING THE CAKE

PROJECT:	*SNACKWELL'S GOLDEN SNACK BARS*	
NUTRITION STATS:	*FAT-1.8g/CAL.-113*	JOB NO. *S5777134-GSB*

RED LOBSTER LEMON-PEPPER GRILLED MAHI-MAHI

The Red Lobster menu describes this dish as: "A mild-tasting fillet sprinkled with lemon-pepper seasoning, plus rice." Simple enough. And, if you keep the butter to a minimum, this clone becomes a naturally low-fat meal. Most of the butter will melt away from the fish when grilling, and mahi-mahi has hardly any fat in it. The liquid smoke is here to give the fish a flavor similar to that served in the restaurant, and I find Jane's brand of lemon-pepper seasoning the best to use here, if you can find it. Add some rice on the side— either brown or converted—some steamed veggies, and you've got yourself an incredibly guilt-free meal.

You may also wish to serve this with the fat-free tartar sauce from page 210.

1 ½ pounds mahi-mahi fillets, skinned
1 tablespoon water
2 to 3 drops liquid smoke

1 tablespoon butter, melted
1 teaspoon lemon-pepper seasoning (Jane's is best)

1. Preheat the barbecue or indoor grill to high heat.
2. Cut the mahi-mahi into four equal portions. Be sure to remove the skin.
3. Combine the water and liquid smoke in a small bowl. Brush this solution over the entire surface of each piece of fish.
4. Brush the melted butter over the entire surface of each piece of fish.

5. Sprinkle a generous portion of the lemon-pepper seasoning on the top of each piece of fish, then grill the fish with this side down on the grill. Sprinkle the remaining seasoning over the top of each piece.
6. Grill the fish for 5 to 6 minutes per side, then serve hot with rice.

- SERVES 2.

Nutrition Facts

SERVING SIZE—2 FILLETS   FAT (PER SERVING)—5G

TOTAL SERVINGS—2   CALORIES (PER SERVING)—340

• • • •

RED LOBSTER NANTUCKET BAKED COD

Here's another Red Lobster selection that is a simple, healthy choice for your next kitchen-cloned meal. The menu described it as: "A flaky, white fish, baked with fresh tomatoes & Parmesan, served with rice." Much of the butter will slip away from the fish, and you will get a very small amount of fat from the Parmesan cheese; but at a total of 6 grams of fat per serving, this is still a very low-fat choice for lunch or dinner. Serve this dish with rice and some steamed veggies, and save the fat grams for dessert.

You may also want to serve this with some of the fat-free tartar sauce from page 210.

SPICE BLEND

¼ teaspoon salt	dash black pepper
¼ teaspoon paprika	dash cayenne pepper

1 ½ pounds fresh cod fillet	2 small tomatoes, thinly sliced
1 tablespoon butter, melted	2 tablespoons grated Parmesan
lemon juice	cheese

1. Combine the spices in a small bowl and set aside.
2. Preheat the oven to 425 degrees. Cut the fish into 4 equal portions (2 per serving), and arrange the fillets in a 9 x 13-inch baking dish or pan.
3. Melt the butter in a small bowl in the microwave for 10 to 20 seconds. Brush the top of each fillet with butter, drizzle a little lemon juice on the fish, then sprinkle the spice blend evenly over the top of each fillet.

4. Arrange 2 to 3 tomato slices over the top of each fillet.
5. Sprinkle grated Parmesan cheese over each tomato slice. Each slice should be at least 50 percent covered with the cheese, and it's okay for some of the cheese to fall on the fish.
6. Bake the fish, uncovered, for 8 minutes, then turn the oven to a high broil and continue to cook for 6 to 8 minutes or until the cheese on the tomatoes begins to brown. Serve two pieces of fish together, with rice on the side.

- SERVES 2.

Nutrition Facts

SERVING SIZE—2 FILLETS

TOTAL SERVINGS—2

FAT (PER SERVING)—6G

CALORIES (PER SERVING)—370

• • • •

SWISS MISS FAT-FREE CHOCOLATE FUDGE PUDDING

Hunt-Wesson first introduced a light variety of Swiss Miss Puddings in 1990, but three years later changed the formula to fat-free. This chocolaty clone of the rich pudding you find in the refrigerated section of the supermarket will satisfy your chocolate craving without contributing any of those nasty fat grams. You'll notice that the sweetened condensed milk helps to replace fat, and the cornstarch jumps in to keep the pudding thick and creamy. Add two types of chocolate and you've got an irresistible snack that tastes just like the real deal.

2½ cups fat-free milk
2 tablespoons unsweetened cocoa
   powder
3 tablespoons cornstarch
½ cup sweetened condensed
   skim milk

3 tablespoons Hershey's chocolate
   syrup
dash salt
½ teaspoon vanilla extract

1. In a saucepan, combine the fat-free milk with the cocoa powder and cornstarch and whisk thoroughly until the powders are dissolved.
2. Add the condensed milk, chocolate syrup, and salt to the saucepan. Set the pan over medium/low heat. Heat the mixture, stirring constantly, until it comes to a boil and then thickens. This will take about 6 minutes.

3. Remove the pan from the heat and let it sit, covered, for 5 minutes. Then add the vanilla.
4. Transfer the pudding to serving cups, cover each with plastic wrap, and chill for at least 2 to 3 hours before serving.

- SERVES 4.

TIDBITS

Cover the pudding tightly when chilling and eat it within a few days or it may begin to thin.

Nutrition Facts

SERVING SIZE—¾ CUP   FAT (PER SERVING)—0G
TOTAL SERVINGS—4   CALORIES (PER SERVING)—170

• • • •

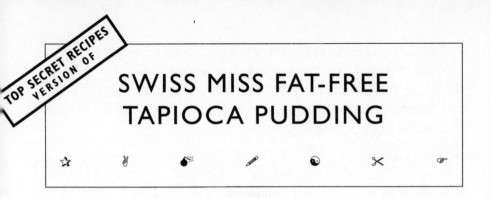

SWISS MISS FAT-FREE TAPIOCA PUDDING

When the first instant hot cocoa mix was developed in the fifties, it was available only to the airlines in individual portions for passengers and was called Brown Swiss. This mix was so popular that the company packaged it for sale in the grocery stores and changed the name to Swiss Miss. In the seventies, the first Swiss Miss Puddings were introduced and quickly became the leader of dairy case puddings. When the fat-free versions of the puddings were introduced some 23 years later, they, too, would become a popular favorite.

No sugar needs to be added to this recipe that recreates one of the best-tasting brands of fat-free pudding on the market. The condensed milk is enough to sweeten the pudding; plus it provides a creamy consistency, which, along with the cornstarch, helps to replace the fat found in the full-fat version of this tasty tapioca treat. It's a simple recipe to make and you won't even "miss" the fat.

2 tablespoons cornstarch
2½ cups fat-free milk
½ cup sweetened condensed
   skim milk

dash salt
2½ tablespoons instant tapioca
½ teaspoon vanilla extract

1. Combine the cornstarch with the fat-free milk in a medium saucepan and whisk thoroughly to dissolve the cornstarch.
2. Add the condensed milk, salt, and tapioca to the pan. Stir until smooth and then set the pan aside for 5 minutes.
3. After 5 minutes, bring the mixture to a boil over medium/low

heat, stirring constantly until it thickens, then cover and remove from the heat. Let the pudding sit, covered, for 20 minutes.

4. Stir in the vanilla, then transfer the pudding to serving cups. Cover the cups with plastic wrap and let them chill for at least 2 to 3 hours before serving.

- SERVES 4.

TIDBITS

Cover the pudding tightly when chilling and eat it within a few days or it may begin to thin.

Nutrition Facts

SERVING SIZE—¾ CUP	FAT (PER SERVING)—0G
TOTAL SERVINGS—4	CALORIES (PER SERVING)—140

• • • •

T.G.I. FRIDAY'S
FAT-FREE CHEESECAKE

For the last couple of years T.G.I. Friday's has been serving a delicious cheesecake drizzled with strawberry sauce. The cheesecake tastes like a decadent, fat-filled dessert; it's creamy and delicious. But the shocker comes when you realize that there is not one gram of fat in a single serving. Many recipes for fat-free cheesecakes produce a cheesecake with an unusual taste or one that is very hard on top. This clone recipe will solve those problems and produce a dessert that tastes like the popular cheesecake you can order at one of America's most successful restaurant chains.

You'll need a 9½-inch springform pan for this recipe, and be sure to let the cream cheese come to room temperature (keep it covered) before you use it. Serve this one to your friends and watch the surprise when you tell them it's 100 percent fat-free.

5 8-ounce pkgs. fat-free
   Philadelphia cream cheese
1¼ cups sugar
⅔ cup fat-free sour cream

2½ tablespoons flour
2 teaspoons vanilla
½ cup egg substitute

CRUST
1 tablespoon ground pecans
3 tablespoons graham cracker
   crumbs

1½ teaspoons sugar
nonstick cooking spray

STRAWBERRY SAUCE
8 ounces frozen strawberries
⅓ cup sugar

2 tablespoons water

---

1. Bring the cream cheese to room temperature. Preheat the oven to 325 degrees.
2. Using an electric mixer, whip the cream cheese in a large bowl until smooth. Add the sugar, sour cream, flour, and vanilla and beat until well incorporated.
3. Add the egg substitute and mix only until combined. Do not overmix once the egg substitute is added.
4. To make the crust, measure the pecans after grinding them up in a food processor or blender, then return them to the processor. Add the graham cracker crumbs and 1½ teaspoons of sugar to the pecans and pulse for about 15 seconds to form a fine meal. Spray the inside of a 9½-inch springform pan with a light coating of cooking spray. Wipe off any excess spray around the top rim of the pan. The spray should only coat the bottom and up about two inches on the sides. Anything sprayed above that can be wiped off. Dump the crumbs into the pan and swirl the pan so that the bottom and sides are coated with the crumbs. Lightly tap out any excess.
5. Pour the cream cheese mixture into the springform pan, being careful not to disturb the crumbs when pouring. Gently spread the cheese mixture close to the edge, but don't touch the sides or you may disturb the crumbs.
6. Bake the cheesecake for 50 to 60 minutes or until the top of the cheesecake is firm. The center may not entirely set until the cheesecake cools. Cover and cool for 2 hours at room temperature, and then refrigerate.
7. As the cheesecake cools, prepare the strawberry sauce by combining the strawberries, sugar, and water in a microwave-safe bowl. Cover, and microwave on 50 percent power for 2 minutes. If the strawberries are still frozen, you may have to heat the mixture for as long as 4 to 5 minutes. Stir to dissolve the sugar, then let stand for 10 to 15 minutes. Pour the mixture into the blender or food processor and puree until smooth. Strain and chill.
8. Cut the cheesecake into 12 slices. Serve each slice with about 1 tablespoon of the strawberry sauce poured over the top.

- SERVES 12.

Nutrition Facts

SERVING SIZE—1 SLICE   FAT (PER SERVING)—0G

TOTAL SERVINGS—12   CALORIES (PER SERVING)—223

• • • •

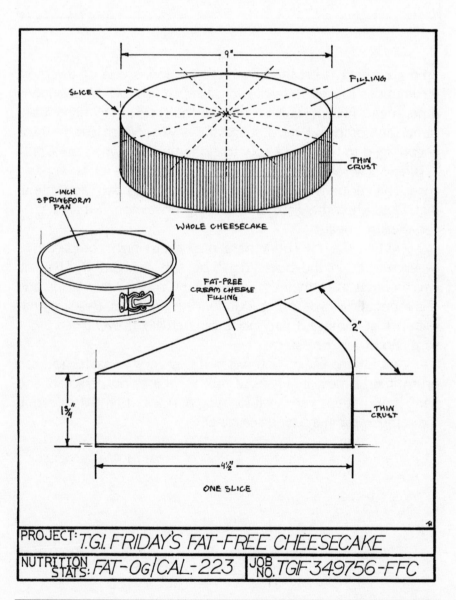

WHOLE CHEESECAKE

ONE SLICE

PROJECT: *T.G.I. FRIDAY'S FAT-FREE CHEESECAKE*

NUTRITION STATS: *FAT-0G/CAL-223*   JOB NO. *TGIF-34-9756-FFC*

T.G.I. FRIDAY'S JACK DANIEL'S GRILL SALMON

The glaze that is brushed over this salmon is one of the most scrumptious sauces you will ever taste on fish, or just about any other meat. T.G.I. Friday's introduced the glaze in 1997 and it became the company's most successful new product launch. I was encouraged to figure out how to clone the stuff when the *Oprah Winfrey Show* requested a recreation of the glaze for an appearance. This recipe is the result of hard work, and darn accurate at that. Plus, when the glaze is brushed over salmon, it makes for a very healthy meal.

    While the fat count here may seem high compared to other recipes in the book, don't be too concerned. That fat, which comes from the salmon, is called Omega-3 fatty acids, and it is a beneficial type of fat found in fish and nuts. Research has shown that Omega-3 fatty acids can actually prevent heart disease and lower cholesterol.

    As for the sauce, you will find it is very versatile. You can brush it on almost any type of fish, as well as ribs, chicken, and beef. It also keeps very well for long periods of time if stored in the refrigerator in a sealed container.

GLAZE

1 head of garlic
1 tablespoon olive oil
²/₃ cup water
1 cup pineapple juice
¼ cup teriyaki sauce
1 tablespoon soy sauce
1 ⅓ cups dark brown sugar

3 tablespoons lemon juice
3 tablespoons minced white
   onion
1 tablespoon Jack Daniel's
   whiskey
1 tablespoon crushed pineapple
¼ teaspoon cayenne pepper

4½-pound fresh Atlantic salmon
   fillets
fat-free butter-flavored spray or
   spread

salt
pepper

1. Preheat the oven to 325 degrees.
2. To roast the garlic for the glaze, cut about ½-inch off the top of the garlic head. Cut the roots so that the garlic will sit flat. Remove most of the papery skin from the garlic, but leave enough so that the cloves stay together. Place the head of garlic in a small casserole dish or baking pan, drizzle the olive oil over it, and cover it with a lid or foil. Bake for 1 hour. Remove the garlic and let it cool until you can handle it.
3. Combine the water, pineapple juice, teriyaki sauce, soy sauce, and brown sugar in a medium saucepan over medium/high heat. Stir occasionally until the mixture boils, then reduce the heat until the mixture is just simmering.
4. Squeeze the sides of the head of garlic until the pasty roasted garlic is squeezed out. Measure 2 teaspoons into the saucepan and whisk to combine. Add the remaining glaze ingredients to the pan and stir.
5. Let the mixture simmer for 40 to 50 minutes or until the glaze has reduced by about one-third and is thick and syrupy. Make sure it doesn't boil over. When the glaze is done, cover the saucepan and set it aside until the fish is ready.
6. To cook the fish, preheat your barbecue or kitchen grill to medium/high heat. Remove any skin or bones from the fillets. Brush the entire surface of each fillet with a light coating of the

fat-free butter-flavored spread or spray. Lightly salt and pepper both sides of the fillets and place them on the hot grill at a slight angle, so that grill marks will be made at an angle on the fish. Cook each fillet for 2 to 4 minutes, then turn them over, placing them back on the grill at an angle once again. After 2 to 4 minutes, turn the fish over at a different angle so that the grill marks will criss-cross. Cook 2 to 4 minutes more, flip again, and cook until done. The entire cooking time should be somewhere between 8 to 15 minutes depending on the thickness of your fillets and the heat of the grill. Be careful not to burn the fish, and quickly move the fish away from any flare-ups.

7. When the fillets are done, remove them from the grill and spoon a generous portion of glaze over each one. Serve hot with a baked potato and vegetables, if desired.

- SERVES 4 AS AN ENTRÉE.

Nutrition Facts

SERVING SIZE—1 FILLET
TOTAL SERVINGS—4

FAT (PER SERVING)—16.5G
CALORIES (PER SERVING)—525

• • • •

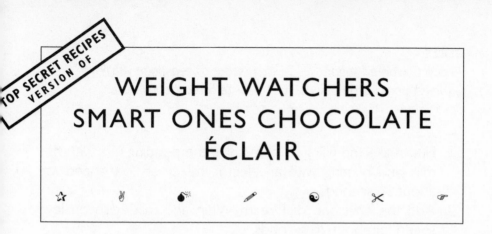

WEIGHT WATCHERS SMART ONES CHOCOLATE ÉCLAIR

Weight Watchers was one of the first companies to introduce low-fat foods to the freezer section of your local supermarket. Those earlier items were mostly meals, such as dinners and lunch items. In 1980, the company began offering a selection of low-fat desserts, which quickly gained in popularity; probably because they didn't taste low-fat. But more recent favorites are these small chocolate-frosted, crème-filled eclairs, developed in 1993. The originals are bought and stored frozen, but they can be defrosted at room temperature within an hour and scarfed down, guilt-free.

The clone recipe here is designed so that you don't need a special pastry bag to make the shells, or to fill them with the delicious, custard-like combination of fat-free vanilla pudding and Dream Whip. It's an éclair recipe you won't find anywhere else, and it's guaranteed to satisfy your most fierce dessert craving.

FILLING

¼ cup instant vanilla pudding
   (½ of a 3.4-ounce package)
⅔ cup fat-free milk

1 envelope Dream Whip
dash salt

SHELLS

1½ cups cake flour, sifted
¼ teaspoon baking powder
1½ cups water
2½ tablespoons butter

¼ teaspoon vanilla
1 tablespoon sugar
dash salt
4 egg whites, slightly beaten

GLAZE

¾ cup powdered sugar · scant ½ teaspoon vanilla
2 tablespoons cocoa powder · 4 to 5 teaspoons water
dash salt

1. First make the filling by combining the pudding mix with the milk and beating with an electric mixer on low speed for about 30 seconds.
2. Add the envelope of Dream Whip and mix again on low speed for about 30 seconds.
3. Turn the mixer speed to high and continue beating the mixture for about 2 minutes until it's light and fluffy. Cover and chill for at least an hour (while you are making the shells).
4. Preheat the oven to 400 degrees.
5. To make the shells, mix the flour and baking powder together in a medium bowl and set aside.
6. Combine the water, butter, vanilla, sugar, and salt in a medium saucepan and bring the mixture to a boil over high heat.
7. Turn the heat down to low and add the flour and baking powder mixture all at once. Stir vigorously with a wooden spoon until the mixture forms a ball and pulls away from the side of the pan. Remove the pan from the heat and immediately transfer the mixture to a medium mixing bowl.
8. Add the 4 egg whites to the bowl. Beat the mixture with a wooden spoon to incorporate the egg whites until it becomes smooth and forms a paste.
9. Make a pastry bag by cutting the corner off a plastic storage bag. Cut about ¾-inch in from the corner to create a hole that is about 1 inch in diameter. Fill the bag with the dough while it is still warm—you don't want the dough to cool.
10. Pipe 4½-inch strips of dough onto an ungreased baking sheet. You should be able to make 9 strips of dough.
11. Bake for 20 to 25 minutes, then reduce the heat to 325 degrees and bake for an additional 30 to 35 minutes until the shells are light brown. Let cool.
12. Cut the tip off one end of each shell and scrape out the soft doughy centers with a cocktail fork or handle end of a spoon.

13. When the inside of the shells have cooled completely, use another bag with a corner cut off (a little smaller hole this time) to fill each one with the chilled filling.
14. Make the chocolate glaze by combining the powdered sugar, cocoa, and salt in a medium bowl. Add the vanilla and 4 teaspoons of water and stir the mixture until it is smooth. If it is too thick, add an additional teaspoon of water.
15. Spread the glaze over the top of each éclair. Serve immediately, or you can freeze the éclairs. If frozen, the éclairs should thaw at room temperature for 1 hour before serving.

• MAKES 9 ÉCLAIRS.

Nutrition Facts

SERVING SIZE—1 ECLAIR   FAT (PER SERVING)—4G
TOTAL SERVINGS—9   CALORIES (PER SERVING)—160

• • • •

TOP SECRET
RECIPES
LITE!
CONVERSIONS

APPLEBEE'S
BAJA POTATO BOATS

This is Applebee's variation on the popular potato skins appetizer made famous by T.G.I. Friday's. Many seem to prefer these to regular potato skins because of their south-of-the-border flair. The only problem is, a serving of the version that you would order in the restaurant has around 12 grams of fat (even more if you glop on the sour cream). And that's for only three pieces. If you usually don't stop there, you may be interested in this TSR version of the delicious dish, which cuts the fat by 66 percent. Now you can eat three times as much of these Mexican-style potato skin wedges for the same amount of fat as the real deal, thanks to reduced-fat cheese and fat-free sour cream.

PICO DE GALLO
1 tomato, chopped (½ cup)
3 tablespoons chopped Spanish
    onion
1 ½ teaspoons minced fresh cilantro

1 tablespoon canned jalapeño
    slices (nacho slices), diced
dash salt
dash pepper

POTATO BOATS
3 medium russet potatoes
canola oil nonstick cooking spray
salt
⅓ cup reduced-fat shredded
    cheddar cheese

⅓ cup reduced-fat shredded
    mozzarella cheese
2 slices Canadian bacon, diced
    (about 2 tablespoons)

ON THE SIDE
fat-free sour cream

salsa

1. Make the pico de gallo by combining the ingredients in a small bowl. Cover and refrigerate until needed.
2. Bake the potatoes at 400 degrees for 1 hour, or until tender, and let cool.
3. When the potatoes are cool enough to handle, make two lengthwise cuts through each potato, resulting in three ½- to ¾-inch slices. Discard the middle slices or save them for a separate dish of mashed potatoes. This will leave you with two whole potato skins per potato.
4. Crank the oven up to 450 degrees.
5. With a spoon, scoop some of the potato out of each skin, being sure to leave about ¼ inch of potato inside of the skin.
6. Spray the entire surface of each potato skin, inside and out, with a light coating of the canola oil spray.
7. Place the skins on a baking sheet, cut side up, salt them, then bake them for 12 to 15 minutes, or until the edges are beginning to brown.
8. Combine the cheeses in a small bowl, then sprinkle about a tablespoon and a half of the cheese blend on each of the potato skins.
9. Sprinkle a teaspoon of Canadian bacon over the cheese on each skin.
10. Spread a heaping tablespoon of pico de gallo over the bacon on each skin.
11. Top off each potato skin with another pinch of the cheese blend.
12. Bake the skins once more for 2 to 4 minutes or until the cheese is melted. Remove the skins from the oven, let them sit for about a minute, then slice each one lengthwise. These are your "boats." Serve them hot with fat-free sour cream and salsa on the side.

• SERVES 4 AS AN APPETIZER.

Nutritional Facts (per serving)
SERVING SIZE—3 PIECES   TOTAL SERVINGS—4

	LITE	ORIGINAL
CALORIES (est.)	246	390
FAT (approx.)	4G	12G

• • • •

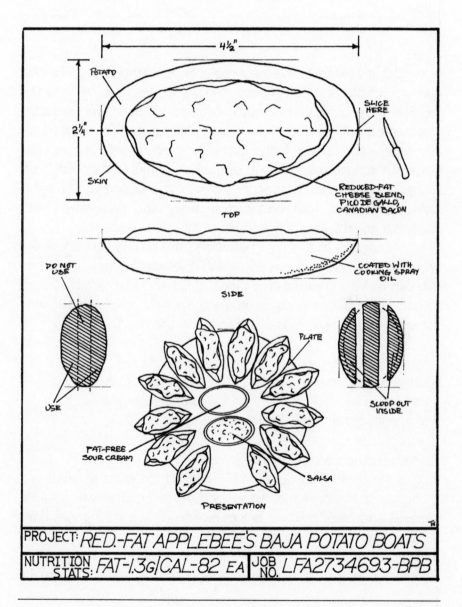

4½"

POTATO

SLICE HERE

2¼"

SKIN

REDUCED-FAT CHEESE BLEND, PICO DE GALLO, CANADIAN BACON

TOP

COATED WITH COOKING SPRAY OIL

SIDE

DO NOT USE

USE

FAT-FREE SOUR CREAM

PLATE

SCOOP OUT INSIDE

SALSA

PRESENTATION

PROJECT: *RED.-FAT APPLEBEE'S BAJA POTATO BOATS*

NUTRITION STATS: *FAT-1.3G/CAL.-82 EA* JOB NO. *LFA2734693-BPB*

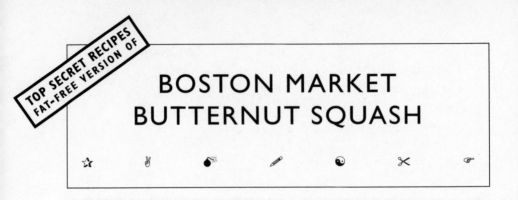

BOSTON MARKET
BUTTERNUT SQUASH

☆   ✌   💣   ✏   ☯   ✂   ☞

In the biz, it's called home meal replacement. And Boston Market was one of the first companies out of the gate to enter into this recently very competitive sector of food service. The company was started in 1989 and offered its special recipe of marinated rotisserie chicken, along with several homestyle side dishes. The butternut squash was not one of the company's first side dish offerings, but has recently become one of the favorites. The light-tasting vegetable, seasoned with nutmeg and sweetened with sugar, is a healthy alternative to more fat-filled fare.

According to the nutrition sheet, the chain's version of this bright yellow side dish has some fat in it—probably from butter. We can make a great fat-free clone of Boston Market's butternut squash, using Butter Buds Sprinkles to replace any fat, along with the same type of spices that are found in the real thing.

1 butternut squash	¼ teaspoon salt
nonstick cooking spray	¼ teaspoon nutmeg
1 tablespoon sugar	¼ teaspoon allspice
2 teaspoons Butter Buds Sprinkles	dash pepper

1. Preheat the oven to 350 degrees.
2. Cut the butternut squash in half and scrape out the seeds and stringy stuff. Spray the cut surface of the squash with cooking spray and place the two halves facedown in a baking pan. Bake for 1 hour, or until tender.
3. Scoop out all of the tender squash and load it into a medium bowl. Use a potato masher to puree the squash. To make

it even smoother, like the original, you may want to run it through a food processor set to puree for about 30 seconds.

4. Add the remaining ingredients and mix well.
5. Reheat the squash in the microwave for 1 to 1½ minutes, or until hot, and serve.

• SERVES 4 AS A SIDE DISH.

Nutritional Facts (per serving)

SERVING SIZE—½ CUP   TOTAL SERVINGS—4

	LITE	ORIGINAL
CALORIES	74	160
FAT	0G	6G

• • • •

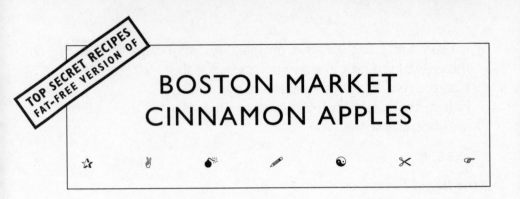
BOSTON MARKET CINNAMON APPLES

By the end of 1997, there were 1,166 Boston Market outlets in 38 states. It took only ten years for the company to reach this number of units—that's some pretty impressive growth. The cinnamon apple side dish has been on the menu since the company opened the doors to its first outlet. The dish from the chain is fairly low in fat—only 4.5 grams of fat per serving—but there is apparently some butter or oil in there. Using the right cooking techniques and some Butter Buds, we can easily take that fat all the way down to zippo, while still getting all of the same great flavors. The most work you'll do here is peeling the apples, a chore that's made easy by whipping out that peeler you use for carrots and potatoes.

3 Golden Delicious apples
2/3 cup water
1/2 tablespoon flour
1 teaspoon cornstarch

2 teaspoons Butter Buds Sprinkles
1/2 cup light brown sugar
1/4 teaspoon cinnamon
dash salt

1. Preheat the oven to 350 degrees.
2. Peel and core the apples. Cut each one into 16 slices and arrange the slices in an 8 x 8-inch baking dish.
3. In a small bowl, combine the water with the flour, cornstarch, and Butter Buds and stir until the dry ingredients are dissolved and not lumpy. Add the brown sugar and cinnamon and stir until smooth.
4. Pour the cinnamon mixture over the apple slices, cover the

dish with foil, and bake for 40 minutes. Stir the apples every 10 minutes.

- SERVES 4.

Nutritional Facts (per serving)
SERVING SIZE—½ CUP   TOTAL SERVINGS—4

	LITE	ORIGINAL
CALORIES	177	250
FAT	0G	4.5G

• • • •

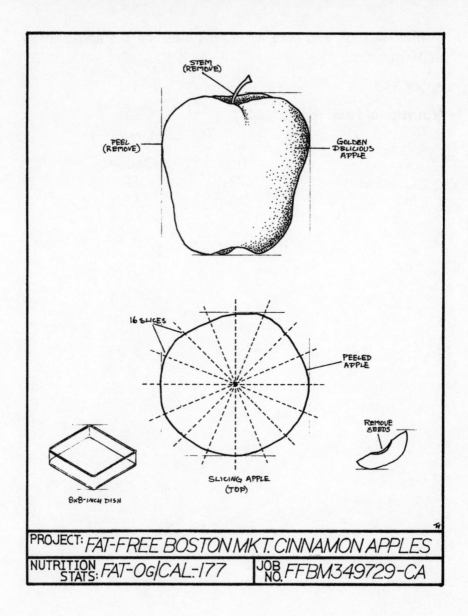

STEM
(REMOVE)

PEEL
(REMOVE)

GOLDEN
DELICIOUS
APPLE

16 SLICES

PEELED
APPLE

REMOVE
SEEDS

SLICING APPLE
(TOP)

8X8-INCH DISH

PROJECT: *FAT-FREE BOSTON MKT. CINNAMON APPLES*

NUTRITION STATS: *FAT-0G/CAL.-177*

JOB NO. *FFBM349729-CA*

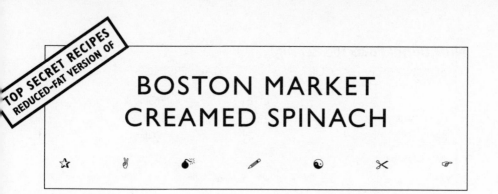

BOSTON MARKET CREAMED SPINACH

When Boston Market first opened in 1989, it was called Boston Chicken. That's because at that time chicken was the only meat served at the chain. But three years later, in 1992, the chain added meatloaf, turkey, and ham, and officially became Boston Market. Yes, a lot of signs had to be changed, at considerable expense.

This popular side dish, which contains three types of cheese, normally has 24 grams of fat per serving. So, for this clone recipe, we'll be using two fat-free cheeses along with regular Provolone, and we'll be able to re-create the taste of the real thing; but with only 25 percent of the fat in the original.

2 10-ounce packages chopped
   frozen spinach
2 tablespoons diced white
   onion
3 ounces provolone cheese,
   chopped

4 slices Kraft fat-free Swiss
   Cheese Singles, quartered
4 slices Kraft fat-free Mozzarella
   Singles, quartered
1 ½ teaspoons white vinegar
¼ heaping teaspoon salt

1. Thaw the spinach and place it in a medium saucepan over medium/low heat with the onion. Heat for 7 to 10 minutes or until the liquid begins to bubble. Drain.
2. Add the remaining ingredients to the saucepan and heat for an additional 5 to 7 minutes or until smooth and creamy.

- SERVES 4.

Nutritional Facts *(per serving)*

SERVING SIZE—½ CUP   TOTAL SERVINGS—4

	LITE	ORIGINAL
CALORIES	180	300
FAT	6G	24G

• • • •

BURGER KING
BK BROILER

Here's a clone for a sandwich that America's number-two burger chain introduced in 1990, and soon after the launch was selling over a million a day. This was the same year that Burger King switched from animal fat to vegetable oil to cook the fried items. But, even though the BK Broiler includes flame-broiled chicken, rather than fried, it still comes in with 29 grams. A big part of that comes from the mayonnaise. So, by replacing the regular mayonnaise with fat-free mayo and by not adding any additional fats, we can produce a sandwich that will taste like a BK Broiler, yet have less than one-quarter of the fat and fewer calories.

MARINADE
¾ cup water
2 teaspoons ketchup
1 teaspoon salt
¼ teaspoon liquid smoke

⅛ teaspoon pepper
⅛ teaspoon oregano
dash onion powder
dash parsley

2 chicken breast fillets
4 sesame seed hamburger buns
1⅓ cups chopped lettuce

¼ cup fat-free mayonnaise
8 tomato slices

1. Make the marinade by combining the ingredients in a medium bowl.
2. Prepare the chicken by cutting each breast in half. Fold a piece of plastic wrap around each piece of chicken and pound the meat with a tenderizing mallet until it is about ¼-inch thick and

about the same diameter as the hamburger buns. Place the chicken in the marinade, cover it, and chill for at least four hours. Overnight is even better.

3. Preheat your barbecue or indoor grill to high heat. Grill the chicken for 3 to 4 minutes per side or until done.
4. Toast the faces of the hamburger buns in a pan or griddle, in a toaster oven, or facedown on the grill. Watch the buns closely to be certain that the faces turn only light brown and do not burn.
5. Build each sandwich from the top down by first spreading about a tablespoon of the fat-free mayonnaise on the toasted face of a top bun.
6. Spread about ⅓ cup of chopped lettuce over the mayonnaise.
7. Arrange two tomato slices on the lettuce.
8. Place a chicken breast on the toasted face of the bottom bun.
9. Flip the top part of the sandwich over onto the bottom and munch out.

• SERVES 4.

Nutritional Facts (per serving)
SERVING SIZE—1 SANDWICH   TOTAL SERVINGS—4

	LITE	ORIGINAL
CALORIES	335	550
FAT	6G	29G

• • • •

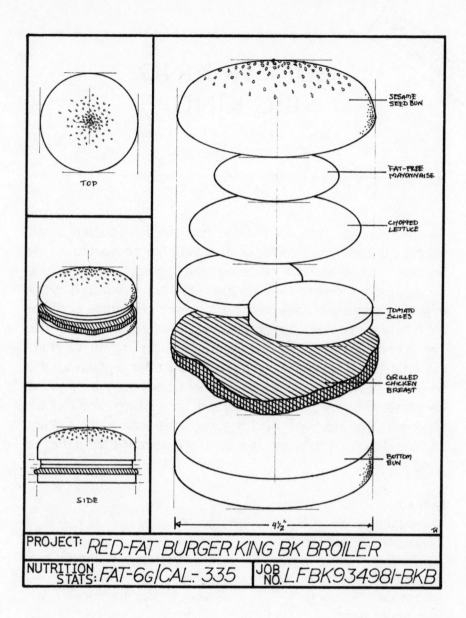

TOP

SIDE

SESAME
SEED BUN

FAT-FREE
MAYONNAISE

CHOPPED
LETTUCE

TOMATO
SLICES

GRILLED
CHICKEN
BREAST

BOTTOM
BUN

4½"

PROJECT: *RED.-FAT BURGER KING BK BROILER*

NUTRITION
STATS: *FAT-6g/CAL.- 335*

JOB
NO. *LFBK93498I-BKB*

BURGER KING
BIG KING

The burger wars are on and the battlefield is splattered with ketchup. Burger King stepped up first with this competitor of the Big Mac. Yes, it has two all-beef patties, special sauce, lettuce, cheese, pickles, onions on a sesame seed bun—although everything's arranged a bit differently, and there's no middle bun. The beef patties are also bigger than those found on a Big Mac. The other big difference? The Big King weighs in with 12 grams more fat than Mickey D's signature product, for a grand total of 43 grams. Now TSR enters into the fray. Check out this clone that re-creates the "secret" burger spread from scratch and includes super-lean ground beef. Add it all up and you've got a gram-zapping clone that comes in at around one-third the fat of the real thing.

SPREAD

¼ cup fat-free mayonnaise
2 teaspoons fat-free French
    dressing
2 teaspoons sweet pickle relish
1 teaspoon white vinegar
½ teaspoon sugar
⅛ teaspoon paprika
1 ½ pounds super-lean ground
    beef (7 percent fat)

dash salt
dash pepper
4 sesame seed hamburger buns
1 ⅓ cups chopped lettuce
8 slices fat-free American
    cheese
1 to 2 slices white onion,
    separated
8 dill pickle slices

1. Prepare the spread by combining the ingredients in a small bowl. Set this aside until you are ready to use it.
2. Preheat your barbecue or indoor grill to high heat.
3. Divide the ground beef into 8 even portions (3 ounces each). Roll each portion into a ball, then press each ball flat to form a patty about the same diameter as the bun.
4. Grill the beef patties for 2 to 3 minutes per side, or until done. Lightly salt and pepper each side of the patties.
5. As the meat cooks, brown the faces of the buns in a hot skillet, toaster oven, or facedown on the grill. Watch the buns closely so that they do not burn.
6. Build each burger by first spreading a tablespoon of the spread on the face of the top bun. Arrange about ⅓ cup of lettuce evenly over the spread.
7. On the bottom bun, stack a patty, then a slice of American cheese, another patty, and another slice of cheese.
8. On the second slice of cheese, arrange 2 to 3 separated onion slices (rings), then 2 pickle slices.
9. Turn the top of the burger over onto the bottom and serve.

- SERVES 4.

Nutritional Facts *(per serving)*

SERVING SIZE—1 SANDWICH   TOTAL SERVINGS—4

	LITE	ORIGINAL
CALORIES	562	660
FAT	15G	43G

. . . .

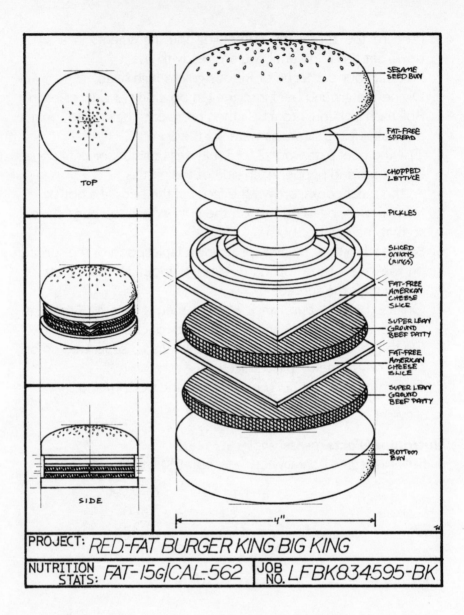

TOP

SIDE

SESAME SEED BUN

FAT-FREE SPREAD

CHOPPED LETTUCE

PICKLES

SLICED ONIONS (RINGS)

FAT-FREE AMERICAN CHEESE SLICE

SUPER LEAN GROUND BEEF PATTY

FAT-FREE AMERICAN CHEESE SLICE

SUPER LEAN GROUND BEEF PATTY

BOTTOM BUN

4"

PROJECT: *RED.-FAT BURGER KING BIG KING*

NUTRITION STATS: *FAT-15G/CAL-562* **JOB NO.** *LFBK834595-BK*

BURGER KING WHOPPER

Burger King's Whopper was an instant hit when it was first introduced in 1957 at a measly 37 cents each. And in more than 9,500 outlets dotting the globe, you can still have the burger "your way"—which comes to over 1,000 different combinations. But by using fat-free mayonnaise and super-lean ground beef, you can still have a sandwich with the taste of Burger King's most popular burger, but with almost 75 percent less in the fat column.

1 sesame seed hamburger bun
1/4-pound super-lean ground beef
   (7 percent fat)
dash salt
dash pepper
1 tablespoon fat-free mayonnaise

1/3 cup chopped lettuce
2 tomato slices
3 to 4 separated onion slices
   (rings)
3 dill pickle slices
1/2 tablespoon ketchup

1. Preheat your barbecue or indoor grill to high.
2. Toast the faces of the sesame seed bun in a hot pan or griddle set to medium heat, in a toaster oven, or facedown on the grill. Keep checking them so that they don't burn.
3. Roll the ground beef into a ball, then flatten it to form a patty about the same diameter as the bun. The patty should be around 1/4-inch thick.
4. Grill the meat on the hot grill for 2 to 3 minutes per side, or until it's done. Lightly salt and pepper each side of the meat.

5. To build the burger start at the top by spreading the mayonnaise onto the toasted face of the top bun.
6. Spread the lettuce on the mayo, then the tomatoes, and onions.
7. Stack the beef patty onto the toasted face of the bottom bun.
8. Arrange the pickles on the beef patty, then spread the ketchup over the pickles.
9. Turn the top of the sandwich over onto the bottom and serve.

• SERVES 1.

Nutritional Facts *(per serving)*
  SERVING SIZE—1 SANDWICH   TOTAL SERVINGS—1

	LITE	ORIGINAL
CALORIES	430	640
FAT	11G	39G

• • • •

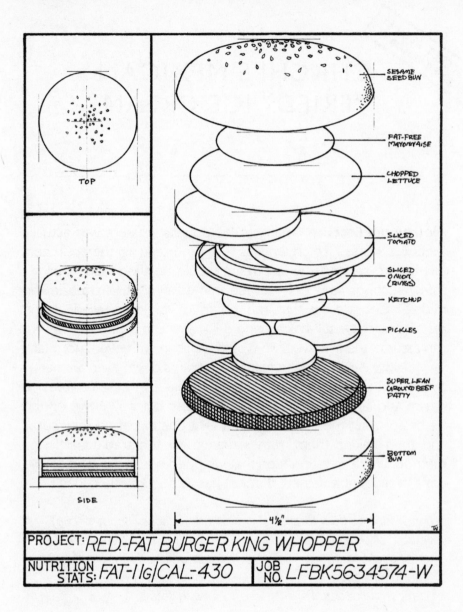

TOP

SIDE

SESAME
SEED BUN

FAT-FREE
MAYONNAISE

CHOPPED
LETTUCE

SLICED
TOMATO

SLICED
ONION
(RINGS)

KETCHUP

PICKLES

SUPER LEAN
GROUND BEEF
PATTY

BOTTOM
BUN

4½"

PROJECT: *RED.-FAT BURGER KING WHOPPER*

NUTRITION
STATS: *FAT-11g/CAL.-430*

JOB
NO. *LFBK5634574-W*

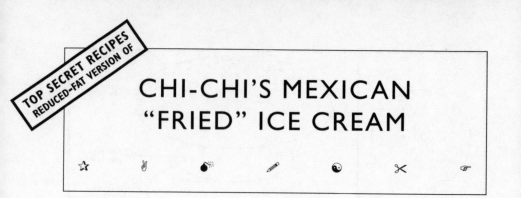

CHI-CHI'S MEXICAN "FRIED" ICE CREAM

At one time the ice cream in this popular dessert was actually fried. A scoop of ice cream was rolled in breading, then refrozen. Just before serving, the ice cream would be flash-fried in oil for a few seconds, and then served immediately, still frozen in the middle. Considering that the nonfried version served at the restaurant chain still has around 34 grams of fat per serving, we can assume the fried version would weigh in with even more fat.

Now we're going to take those grams down even further—by an amazing 80 percent! We'll do that by using fat-free ice cream and fat-free flour tortillas. We'll also cut way down on the fat by spraying the tortillas with a light coating of cooking spray and then baking them, rather than using the traditional frying method. Use a light touch on that whipped cream can, and you've got a very low-fat dessert that just has to be experienced.

2 6-inch fat-free flour tortillas
vegetable oil cooking spray
½ teaspoon cinnamon
2 tablespoons sugar
¼ cup cornflake crumbs

2 large scoops (about ¾ cup)
    fat-free vanilla ice cream
1 can whipped light cream
2 maraschino cherries,
    with stems

OPTIONAL TOPPINGS
Honey
Hershey's chocolate syrup
    (fat-free)

Strawberry topping

1. Preheat the oven to 375 degrees.
2. Spray both sides of each tortilla with a light coating of cooking spray. Place the tortillas on a baking sheet and bake for 10 to 12 minutes, or until the tortillas are golden brown and crispy. Turn the tortillas over halfway through the cooking time.
3. Combine the cinnamon and sugar in a small bowl.
4. Sprinkle half of the cinnamon mixture over both sides of each tortilla, coating evenly. Not all of the cinnamon/sugar will stick to the tortilla, and that's okay.
5. Combine the cornflake crumbs with the remaining cinnamon mixture. Pour this mixture into a large, shallow bowl or onto a plate.
6. Place a large scoop of the fat-free ice cream into the cornflake mixture, and, with your hands, roll the ice cream around until the entire surface of the ice cream is evenly coated.
7. Place the coated scoop of ice cream onto the center of a cinnamon/sugar-coated tortilla.
8. Spray a few small piles of whipped cream around the base of the ice cream, then spray an additional bit of whipped cream on top of the ice cream.
9. Place a cherry into the whipped cream on top. Repeat the process, using the second tortilla. Serve immediately, with a side dish of honey, fat-free chocolate syrup, or strawberry sauce, if desired.

- SERVES 2.

Nutritional Facts (per serving)

SERVING SIZE—1 DESSERT   TOTAL SERVINGS—2

	LITE	ORIGINAL
CALORIES (est.)	371	611
FAT (est.)	7G	34G

• • • •

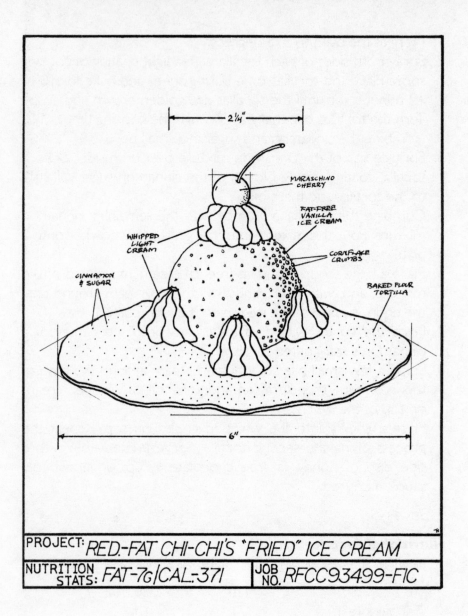

2¼"

MARASCHINO
CHERRY

FAT-FREE
VANILLA
ICE CREAM

WHIPPED
LIGHT
CREAM

CORNFLAKE
CRUMBS

CINNAMON
& SUGAR

BAKED FLOUR
TORTILLA

6"

PROJECT: RED.-FAT CHI-CHI'S "FRIED" ICE CREAM

NUTRITION STATS: FAT-7G/CAL.-371   JOB NO. RFCC93499-FIC

134

CHI-CHI'S
SWEET CORN CAKE

A deserted Kroger grocery store in Richfield, Minnesota, was the site for the first Chi-Chi's in 1976. That was the year restaurateur Marno McDermott got together with ex-Green Bay Packer football player Max McGee to open the first of what would soon become a growing chain of Mexican food restaurants. Today, with around 100 restaurants found mostly in the Midwestern and Eastern states, Chi-Chi's has become famous for its large portions of food, and for the expression, "Don't touch the plate, it's very hot!"

Alongside many of the entrees served at the restaurant is this sweet side dish. It's sort of like a combination of custard and cornbread, with corn and cornmeal in it. But the original is loaded with butter. That means if you eat just a very small scoop of the tasty corn cake you'll be putting away around a dozen fat grams. By using light butter or margarine and substituting milk for the heavy cream, we knock those fat grams down to about half of the real thing served in the restaurant. Yet the flavor and texture is just as good.

½ cup (1 stick) light butter or
    margarine, softened
⅓ cup masa harina
¼ cup water
1 ½ cups frozen corn, thawed

¼ cup cornmeal
⅓ cup sugar
3 tablespoons whole milk
¼ teaspoon salt
½ teaspoon baking powder

1. Preheat the oven to 375 degrees.
2. Blend the butter or margarine in a medium bowl with an electric mixer until creamy. Add the masa harina and water to the butter and beat until well combined.
3. Put the defrosted corn into a blender or food processor and, with short pulses, coarsely chop the corn on low speed. You want to leave several whole kernels of corn. Stir the chopped corn into the butter and masa harina mixture. Add the cornmeal to the mixture. Combine.
4. In another medium bowl, mix together the sugar, milk, salt, and baking powder. When the ingredients are well blended, pour the mixture into the other bowl and stir everything together by hand.
5. Pour the corn batter into an ungreased 8 x 8-inch baking pan. Smooth the surface of the batter with a spatula. Cover the pan with aluminum foil. Place this pan into a 13 x 9-inch pan filled one-third of the way up with hot water. Bake for 50 to 60 minutes or until the corn cake is cooked through.
6. When the corn cake is done, remove the small pan from the larger pan and let it sit for at least 10 minutes. To serve, scoop out each portion with an ice cream scoop or rounded spoon.

• SERVES 8 AS A SIDE DISH.

Nutritional Facts (per serving)
SERVING SIZE—1 SCOOP   TOTAL SERVINGS—8

	LITE	ORIGINAL
CALORIES (est.)	125	185
FAT (est.)	6.5G	13G

• • • •

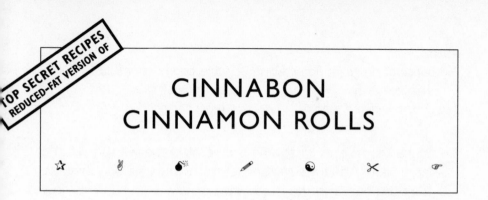

CINNABON
CINNAMON ROLLS

How sinfully delicious are these cinnamon rolls? Their intoxicating aroma wafts through shopping malls and airports all over America, and at one time or another you've probably been a victim of that irresistible, gooey swirl of delight. Sometimes, though, for a treat this delicious, you just have to say "What the heck!" Right? There's a good chance that same thought has gone through the minds of millions since the first Cinnabon was served at Seattle's Sea-Tac Mall in 1985. But what if you could still get that marvelous Cinnabon taste with better than an 80 percent reduction in fat? Not possible, you say? Get out the rolling pin and prepare for an amazing reduced-fat conversion of America's favorite mall food.

ROLLS

1 ¼-ounce package active dry
    yeast
1 cup warm fat-free milk
    (105 to 110 degrees)
½ cup sugar

¼ cup butter
6 tablespoons egg substitute
1 teaspoon salt
4 cups all-purpose flour

FILLING

1 cup dark brown sugar, packed
⅓ cup Wondra flour

2½ tablespoons cinnamon
½ cup fat-free butter spread

ICING

1 8-ounce package fat-free cream
  cheese
1 ½ cups powdered sugar

1 tablespoon Butter Buds
½ teaspoon vanilla
⅛ teaspoon salt

1. Make the rolls by dissolving the yeast in the warm milk in a large bowl. Add the sugar and let the mixture sit for 5 minutes.
2. Melt the butter in the microwave or in a saucepan over low heat and add it to the mixture in the large bowl.
3. Add the egg substitute, salt, and flour to the large bowl, mix to incorporate the ingredients, then use flour-dusted hands to knead the dough into a large ball. Put the dough back into the bowl, cover it, and let it rise in a warm place for about 1 hour, or until it has doubled in size.
4. Make the filling by combining the brown sugar, Wondra flour, and cinnamon in a small bowl. Preheat the oven to 400 degrees.
5. Roll the dough out onto a lightly floured surface. Roll the dough into a flat rectangle until it is approximately 21 inches long and 16 inches wide. It should be about ¼-inch thick.
6. Spread ½ cup of the butter-flavored spread over the surface of the dough. Sprinkle the brown sugar and cinnamon mixture over the spread.
7. Working from the top (a 21-inch side), roll the dough down to the bottom edge.
8. Cut the rolled dough into 1¾-inch slices and place 6, evenly spaced, into each of two 9 x 13-inch lightly greased baking pans. Cover the baking pans and let the rolls rise for another 45 to 60 minutes, then bake for 15 to 22 minutes or until the rolls are light brown on top.
9. While the rolls bake, combine the icing ingredients in a medium bowl and beat well with an electric mixer at high speed until smooth and creamy.
10. Cool the rolls for 3 to 5 minutes after removing them from the oven, then spread icing over the top of each one.

• MAKES 1 DOZEN ROLLS.

Nutritional Facts *(per serving)*

SERVING SIZE—1 ROLL   TOTAL SERVINGS—12

	LITE	ORIGINAL
CALORIES	370	730
FAT	4G	24G

• • • •

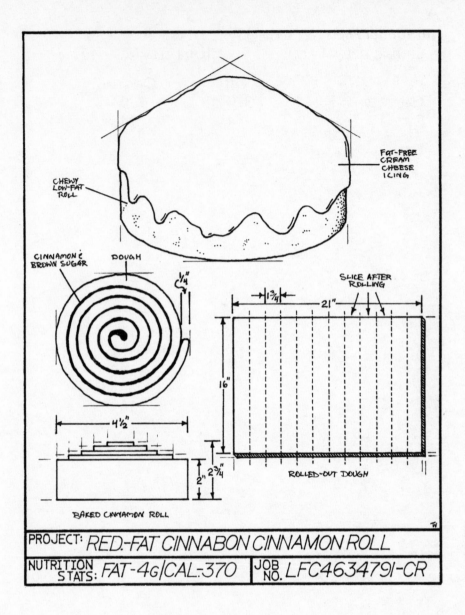

FAT-FREE CREAM CHEESE ICING

CHEWY LOW-FAT ROLL

CINNAMON & BROWN SUGAR

DOUGH

¼"

SLICE AFTER ROLLING

1¾"

21"

16"

4½"

2" 2¾"

ROLLED-OUT DOUGH

BAKED CINNAMON ROLL

TW

PROJECT: *RED.-FAT CINNABON CINNAMON ROLL*

NUTRITION STATS: *FAT-4g/CAL.-370*

JOB NO. *LFC4634791-CR*

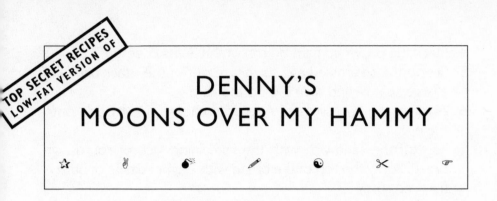

DENNY'S
MOONS OVER MY HAMMY

☆   ✌   💣   ✏   ☯   ✂   ☞

It's got a goofy name and tons of fans. This is one of Denny's most popular sandwiches, and it has remained on Denny's menu since 1978. But whether you have it for breakfast, lunch, or dinner, you might like to know there's a way to enjoy the taste of this grilled sandwich for around 30 grams less fat than the real thing. This TSR version saves grams in several ways, but the most significant savings come from using fat-free cheese. Get some low-fat ham at your supermarket deli counter, or you can find it prepackaged near the luncheon meats. Start heating up a skillet and get ready to discover this delicious lower-fat treat.

½ cup egg substitute
salt
2 ounces low-fat
    deli-sliced ham
2 large slices sourdough bread

fat-free butter-flavored spray
2 slices Kraft Fat-Free Swiss
    Cheese Singles
2 slices Kraft Fat-Free American
    Cheese Singles

1. Preheat two skillets over medium heat. Lightly coat one skillet with cooking spray, then pour the egg substitute into the pan and scramble the egg, cooking it until done. Salt to taste. In the other skillet brown the stack of sliced ham without separating the slices.
2. When the stack of sliced ham has browned lightly on both sides, remove it from the pan. Spray one side of one slice of sourdough bread with the butter-flavored spray, and place it in the hot pan, sprayed side down, to grill.
3. Immediately place the two slices of Swiss cheese side-by-side onto the unbuttered side of the grilling sourdough bread slice.

4. Stack the browned ham on top of the Swiss cheese.
5. Scoop the scrambled egg substitute out of the other pan with a large spatula and slide it onto the ham.
6. Arrange the two slices of American cheese side-by-side onto the egg.
7. Top off the sandwich with the remaining slice of sourdough bread. Spray the top of the bread with a light coating of butter-flavored spray.
8. By this time the bottom surface of the bread in the pan will have browned. Carefully flip the sandwich over to grill the other side for about 2 minutes or until golden brown.
9. Slice the sandwich diagonally through the middle and serve hot.

- MAKES 1 SANDWICH.

Nutritional Facts (per serving)
SERVING SIZE—1 SANDWICH   TOTAL SERVINGS—1

	LITE	ORIGINAL
CALORIES (est.)	460	700
FAT (est.)	3G	33G

• • • •

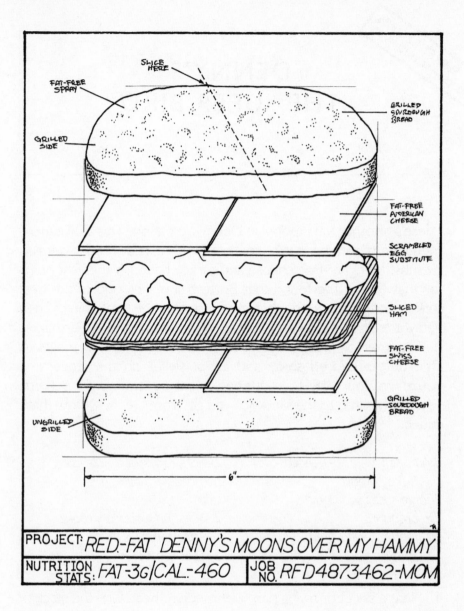

SLICE HERE

FAT-FREE SPRAY

GRILLED SIDE

GRILLED SOURDOUGH BREAD

FAT-FREE AMERICAN CHEESE

SCRAMBLED EGG SUBSTITUTE

SLICED HAM

FAT-FREE SWISS CHEESE

GRILLED SOURDOUGH BREAD

UNGRILLED SIDE

6"

PROJECT: *RED.-FAT DENNY'S MOONS OVER MY HAMMY*

NUTRITION STATS: *FAT-3G/CAL.-460*

JOB NO. *RFD4873462-MOM*

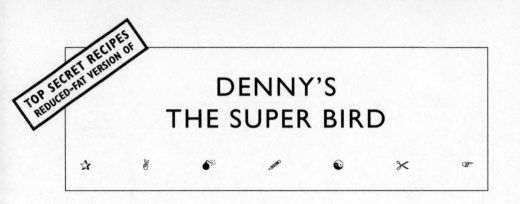

DENNY'S
THE SUPER BIRD

Here's another very popular Denny's creation. This 20-year-old menu item can be easily converted to a reduced-fat version by substituting fat-free cheese and turkey bacon. When shopping for that bacon, I've found that Butterball makes one of the best turkey bacons around—it tastes just like the real thing. Then get yourself some low-fat turkey breast from the supermarket deli counter or prepackaged near the other luncheon meats. A little butter-flavored spray and a hot skillet on the stove, and you're on your way to reducing the fat by around 60 percent, when compared to the sandwich you get from Denny's. Now that's super.

3 ounces low-fat deli-sliced
    turkey breast
2 large slices sourdough
    bread
fat-free butter-flavored
    spray

2 slices Kraft fat-free Swiss
    Cheese Singles
salt
2 slices turkey bacon, cooked
    (Butterball is best)
2 slices tomato

1. Heat a skillet or frying pan over medium heat. Grill the stack of turkey breast in the pan, without separating the stack, until the meat is light brown on both sides.
2. While the turkey is browning, lightly coat one side of a slice of bread with the butter-flavored spray. Place the bread, sprayed side down, in the pan next to the turkey to grill.
3. Arrange the slices of cheese on the face-up, unbuttered side of the bread in the pan.

4. When the turkey has browned, arrange it on top of the cheese. Salt the turkey to taste.
5. Arrange the cooked bacon side-by-side on top of the turkey.
6. Stack the tomato slices side-by-side on top of the bacon.
7. Top off the sandwich with the remaining slice of sourdough bread. Spray a light coating of butter-flavored spray over the surface of the top slice of bread.
8. When the surface of the bottom slice of bread has grilled to a light brown, flip the sandwich over to grill the top for about 2 minutes or until golden brown.
9. With a sharp knife, slice the sandwich twice at a slight angle, creating three equal-size slices. Serve hot.

- MAKES 1 SANDWICH.

Nutritional Facts (per serving)
SERVING SIZE—1 SANDWICH   TOTAL SERVINGS—1

	LITE	ORIGINAL
CALORIES (approx.)	425	565
FAT (approx.)	8.5G	22G

• • • •

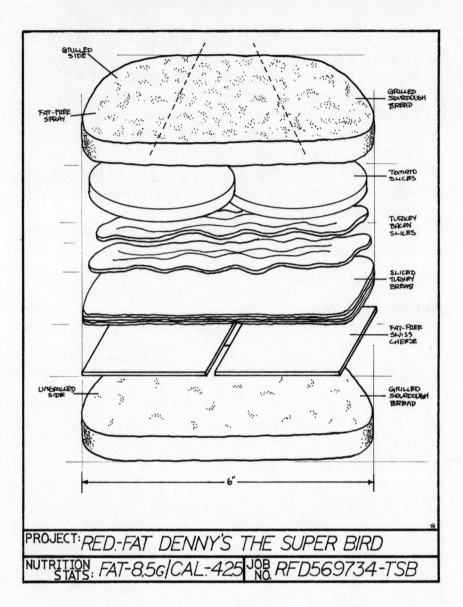

GRILLED SIDE

GRILLED SOURDOUGH BREAD

FAT-FREE SPRAY

TOMATO SLICES

TURKEY BACON SLICES

SLICED TURKEY BREAST

FAT-FREE SWISS CHEESE

UNGRILLED SIDE

GRILLED SOURDOUGH BREAD

6"

PROJECT: *RED.-FAT DENNY'S THE SUPER BIRD*

NUTRITION STATS: *FAT-8.5G/CAL.-425*   JOB NO. *RFD569734-TSB*

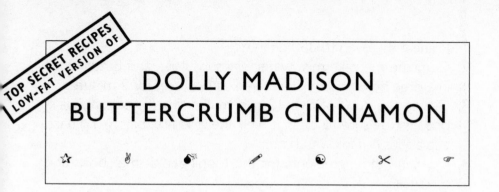

DOLLY MADISON
BUTTERCRUMB CINNAMON

When Interstate Brands started the Dolly Madison line of baked goods that has today become the convenience store leader, it was known as Interstate Bakeries. Roy Nafziger started the bakery in 1927, and he could only have dreamed that one day his company would ring up more than one billion dollars in sales. One item that contributes to those impressive sales figures are these little brown sugar/cinnamon–topped cakes, which have become a popular addition to the Dolly Madison line of baked goods since the late eighties.

We can easily create a low-fat home clone of the real thing with only seven ingredients, thanks to white cake mix that can be found in practically all stores. Notice that the cake mix is not a reduced-fat variety. That's not necessary for the recipe to produce little cakes that taste just like the real thing, but still have less than one-third the fat. And even though the original is sort of square-shaped, we'll use a couple of 12-cup muffin pans to simplify the process. The shape will be different, but the flavor will be right on.

1 18.25-ounce box white cake mix	½ cup egg substitute
1 ¼ cups water	1 tablespoon Butter Buds Sprinkles

TOPPING

⅔ cup dark brown sugar	1 tablespoon cinnamon
2 tablespoons sugar	

1. Preheat the oven to 350 degrees.
2. Combine the cake mix, water, egg substitute, and Butter Buds in a large bowl and mix with an electric mixer for 2 minutes.
3. Grease the cups of two 12-cup muffin tins (if you only have one, just be sure to clean it well after the first batch). Fill each cup about half full with batter.
4. Combine the ingredients for the topping in a small bowl and mix well.
5. Sprinkle about 2 teaspoons of the topping over the batter in each cup. Use a knife to slightly swirl the topping into the batter.
6. Bake the cakes for 20 to 25 minutes or until light brown on top. Store the cakes in a sealed container after they have cooled to keep them fresh.

- MAKES 24 CAKES.

Nutritional Facts (per serving)

SERVING SIZE—1 CAKE   TOTAL SERVINGS—24

	LITE	ORIGINAL
CALORIES	111	170
FAT	1.7G	6G

• • • •

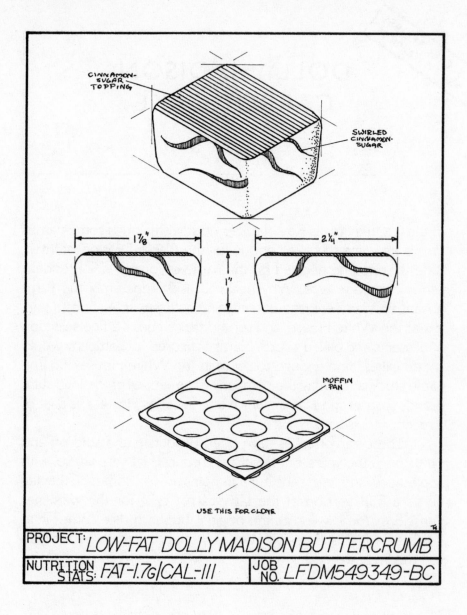

CINNAMON-
SUGAR-
TOPPING

SWIRLED
CINNAMON-
SUGAR

1 7/8"

2 1/4"

1"

MUFFIN
PAN

USE THIS FOR CLONE

PROJECT: *LOW-FAT DOLLY MADISON BUTTERCRUMB*

NUTRITION STATS: *FAT-1.7g/CAL.-111*

JOB NO. *LFDM549349-BC*

DOLLY MADISON
CARROT CAKE

In the late thirties, as Roy Nafziger noodled through some names for his new line of baked goods for the Cakes Division of Interstate Bakeries, he decided on the name of former U.S. President James Madison's wife. Why her, you ask? Apparently the flamboyant first lady enjoyed entertaining guests with elaborate parties at the White House, and served those guests a fine selection of desserts and baked goods. Nafziger figured his company would create cakes "fine enough to serve in the White House." So, the name stuck, and today the company is a member of the Interstate Brands Corporation family, which also includes Hostess as part of a recent acquisition.

These carrot cakes have been produced and sold off and on through the years, but never as a reduced-fat version. So, with applesauce and egg substitute jumping in for some of the fat, here's a TSR version of the tasty carrot cake for the waistline-conscious. You'll swear it's the original, but each slice comes in at less than 4 grams. Even with butter in the icing, that's better than half the fat of the real thing.

1 ⅓ cups sugar
⅔ cup unsweetened applesauce
⅓ cup egg substitute
1 tablespoon canola oil
1 teaspoon white vinegar
½ teaspoon salt
¼ teaspoon vanilla
½ teaspoon cinnamon

¼ teaspoon allspice
⅛ teaspoon ground clove
dash ground ginger
1 ½ cups all-purpose flour
½ cup graham cracker crumbs
1 teaspoon baking soda
1 ⅓ cups grated carrot

ICING

¼ cup fat-free cream cheese (⅓ of an 8-ounce package)	½ teaspoon vanilla
	⅛ teaspoon salt
2 tablespoons butter, softened	3 cups powdered sugar

1. Preheat the oven to 325 degrees.
2. Combine the sugar, applesauce, egg substitute, oil, vinegar, salt, and vanilla in a large bowl and beat by hand.
3. Add the cinnamon, allspice, clove, and ginger and combine.
4. Add the flour, graham cracker crumbs, and baking soda and mix by hand for about 30 strokes.
5. Add the grated carrot and mix just until the carrot is well combined.
6. Pour the batter into a greased 9 x 13-inch baking pan, and bake for 30 to 35 minutes.
7. While the cake is baking, prepare the icing by creaming together the fat-free cream cheese, butter, vanilla, and salt with an electric mixer in a medium bowl. Add the powdered sugar, 1 cup at a time, to the mixture and continue to mix until smooth and creamy.
8. When the cake is done, turn it out of the pan onto a large piece of wax paper. Flip the cake over onto a cooling rack, and after it has cooled for about 15 minutes, peel away the wax paper. This will remove some of the top surface of the cake, allowing the icing to stick.
9. Slice the cake lengthwise down the middle, and then across five times, creating ten equal slices.

• SERVES 10.

Nutritional Facts (per serving)

SERVING SIZE—1 SLICE   TOTAL SERVINGS—10

	LITE	ORIGINAL
CALORIES	520	360
FAT	3.5G	8G

• • • •

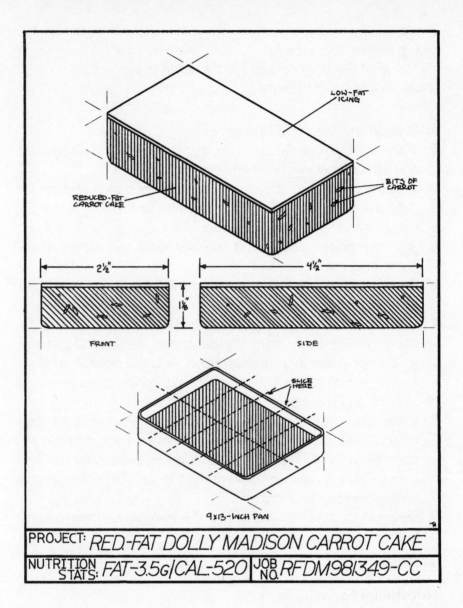

LOW-FAT ICING

BITS OF CARROT

REDUCED-FAT CARROT CAKE

2½"

4½"

1⅛"

FRONT

SIDE

SLICE HERE

9x13-INCH PAN

PROJECT: RED.-FAT DOLLY MADISON CARROT CAKE

NUTRITION STATS: FAT-3.5G/CAL-520

JOB NO. RFDM981349-CC

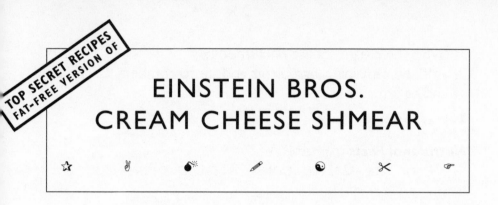

EINSTEIN BROS.
CREAM CHEESE SHMEAR

The Einstein/Noah Bagel Corporation sold around 300 million bagels in 1997—around 6 million bagels a week. And on top of those bagels, customers will smear (or Shmear) more than 8 million pounds of the flavored cream cheeses created by the company. That's 11 tons of the stuff each day! The bagels themselves are reasonably low in fat—coming in at 1 to 3 grams each. But when you add just an ounce of cream cheese Shmear, you're quadrupling the fat, at the very least.

With fat-free cream cheese and a variety of different flavorings and ingredients, we can easily recreate Einstein Bros. Shmear, while reducing the fat to zero. These spreads are very easy to make, and if you would like yours to firm up more after mixing in the ingredients, just pop the finished spread in the microwave (in a microwave-safe bowl) for a minute or two, stir, cover, and chill completely. Use these spreads with bagels of your choice, or with those made in the clone recipes from pages 37 to 44.

ROASTED GARLIC

1 8-ounce tub Philadelphia
   fat-free cream cheese,
   softened
1 ½ teaspoons Lawry's garlic
   spread concentrate

¼ teaspoon dried parsley
   flakes
⅛ teaspoon salt
2 drops yellow food coloring

1. Whip the cream cheese until smooth.
2. Add the remaining ingredients and stir to combine. Cover and chill to firm.

- MAKES 1 CUP.

Nutritional Facts (per serving)
    SERVING SIZE—2 TABLESPOONS   TOTAL SERVINGS—ABOUT 8

	LITE	ORIGINAL
CALORIES	35	100
FAT	0G	9G

STRAWBERRY

1 8-ounce tub Philadelphia
    fat-free cream cheese,
    softened
3 tablespoons sugar

¾ teaspoon strawberry
    extract
1 drop red food coloring

1. Whip the cream cheese until smooth.
2. Add the remaining ingredients and stir to combine. Let the mixture sit for about 5 minutes, then stir again. Cover and chill to firm.

- MAKES 1 CUP.

Nutritional Facts (per serving)
    SERVING SIZE—2 TABLESPOONS   TOTAL SERVINGS—ABOUT 8

	LITE	ORIGINAL
CALORIES	35	100
FAT	0G	8G

JALAPEÑO SALSA

1 8-ounce tub Philadelphia fat-free
   cream cheese, softened
¼ cup Pace medium picante
   salsa

1 teaspoon minced jalapeño
   (nacho slices)
dash salt

1. Whip the cream cheese until smooth.
2. Add the remaining ingredients and mix to combine.
3. Heat the mixture in the microwave for 3 minutes in 1-minute intervals on full power, stirring after each minute. This will help the cream cheese to set up.

- MAKES APPROXIMATELY 1¼ CUPS.

Nutritional Facts (per serving)
   SERVING SIZE—2 TABLESPOONS   TOTAL SERVINGS—ABOUT 10

	LITE	ORIGINAL
CALORIES	30	90
FAT	0G	8G

MAPLE WALNUT RAISIN

1 8-ounce tub Philadelphia
   fat-free cream cheese,
   softened
2 teaspoons chopped walnuts
2 teaspoons raisins

1 teaspoon water
3½ tablespoons dark brown
   sugar, packed
⅛ teaspoon maple flavoring
dash cinnamon

1. Whip the cream cheese until smooth.
2. Grind the walnuts into coarse pieces in a food processor. Remove and set aside.
3. Add the raisins and water to the food processor and chop on high speed until the raisins are cut into much smaller pieces.
4. Combine 1 teaspoon of the ground walnuts and 1 teaspoon of the chopped raisins to the cream cheese. Add the remaining ingredients and mix well. Cover and chill until firm.

- MAKES 1 CUP.

Nutritional Facts (per serving)
   SERVING SIZE—2 TABLESPOONS   TOTAL SERVINGS—ABOUT 8

	LITE	ORIGINAL
CALORIES	48	100
FAT	0G	9G

• • • •

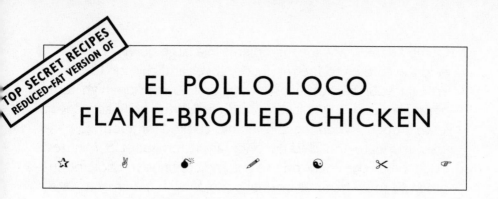

EL POLLO LOCO
FLAME-BROILED CHICKEN

This young chain of Mexican-style chicken outlets has had much success with its formula since the first store opened in the U.S. in 1980. Your order of chicken comes straight off of an open-flame grill, where it has been slowly roasting for around 45 minutes. The chicken is grilled whole, butterfly-style, and before it's boxed up for carry-out, cooks take a sharp hatchet to it in dramatic fashion. A couple of whacks and you're on your way with several pieces of very tasty and tender double-marinated chicken.

For this recipe, instead of butterflying the whole chicken, we will prepare precut pieces. Then, to save on fat grams, as soon as it's cooked, we'll remove the skin. At the restaurant, you're served flour or corn tortillas to wrap around chicken that you strip from the bone. You also get salsa and some side orders to put in the tortilla, if you choose, and I have included clone recipes for salsa, pinto beans, and rice as well (on pages 55, 159, and 160).

This recipe is improved from the version that appears in *More Top Secret Recipes*, so next time you want to clone El Pollo Loco, with or without skin, this is the recipe to use.

MARINADE

4 cups water
2 tablespoons salt
½ teaspoon pepper
2 teaspoons lemon juice

½ cup orange juice
1 large clove garlic, minced
¼ teaspoon yellow food
   coloring

½ roasting chicken, cut into pieces

1. Combine the marinade ingredients in a large bowl.
2. Add the chicken to the marinade, cover, and chill for 1 hour.
3. Preheat your barbecue or indoor grill to medium/high temperature. Cook the chicken on the grill. If the grill has a cover, leave it open. When the chicken has cooked for about 25 minutes, marinate the chicken once again for about 5 minutes. Place the chicken back on the grill and continue to cook for another 20 to 25 minutes or until done. Watch the chicken carefully so that it does not flare up and burn.
4. Before serving the chicken, remove the skin, and serve with steamed flour or corn tortillas—low-fat or fat-free, if you prefer—and with salsa from page 55. You may also wish to serve the chicken with side dishes of pinto beans (page 159) and rice (page 160). You can use this recipe in several of the burritos from pages 161 to 163.

Nutritional Facts (per serving)

SERVING SIZE—2 PIECES   TOTAL SERVINGS—2
  (4.5 OUNCES)

	LITE	ORIGINAL
CALORIES	220	270
FAT	8.5G	14.5G

• • • •

EL POLLO LOCO
PINTO BEANS

This is a simple little recipe that is healthy and delicious. Along with your chicken order from this fast-growing West Coast chain, comes your choice of side orders. Pinto beans is the most popular choice. But the real thing has some fat that you won't need to include in this light version. And this recipe will give you pintos that taste just like the original, down to the little zing in there from finely minced jalapeño pepper. Spoon some of these beans into a tortilla along with the chicken made from the recipe on page 157. Or you may just want to eat them on the side with that chicken recipe, or any other dish.

1 15-ounce can pinto beans,
    with liquid
dash salt

1 teaspoon finely minced fresh
    jalapeño

1. Combine all the ingredients in a small saucepan over medium heat.
2. Bring the beans to a boil, then reduce the heat and simmer for 5 minutes.

• SERVES 4.

Nutritional Facts (per serving)
    SERVING SIZE—½ CUP   TOTAL SERVINGS—4

	LITE	ORIGINAL
CALORIES	96	145
FAT	0G	3G

• • • •

EL POLLO LOCO
SPANISH RICE

☆   ✄   💣   ✎   ☯   ✂   ☞

Here's another clone for a dish served with your chicken from El Pollo Loco. We're gonna use our own culinary magic to cut the fat and create a delicious version of this Spanish rice that still has all of the flavor of the popular original side dish. Be sure that you get converted rice for this one—instant just won't cut it. Then you can use this side in the tortilla with your chicken from page 157, or in many of the burrito recipes on pages 161 to 163. It also makes a great side dish for any other Mexican meal.

1 ½ cups water
1 cup converted rice (not instant)
1 cup tomato sauce
1 ½ tablespoons finely minced onion
2 teaspoons finely minced green
    bell pepper

2 teaspoons finely minced red
    bell pepper
½ teaspoon salt
½ teaspoon chili powder
¼ teaspoon oregano

1. Combine all the ingredients in a medium saucepan over high heat.
2. Bring the mixture to a boil, then reduce the heat and simmer the rice for 20 to 25 minutes, or until the rice is tender.

- SERVES 4.

Nutritional Facts (per serving)
    SERVING SIZE—¾ CUP   TOTAL SERVINGS—4

	LITE	ORIGINAL
CALORIES	187	155
FAT	0G	4G

EL POLLO LOCO
BURRITOS

Here's where we tie it all together. In 1992, to meet the needs of its expanding customer base, El Pollo Loco added several different burrito selections to its menu. The burrito combinations were designed to be assembled with several prepared products the chain had been serving from the start. Here are TSR low-fat versions of four of the most popular burritos, using dishes that are made in the recipes from pages 157 through 160. The fat savings are significant, since the beans and rice are now fat-free, and the recipes use fat-free tortillas and fat-free shredded cheddar cheese. You may also want to add a salsa of your choice to these burritos, or you can use the El Pollo Loco clone recipe from page 55.

B.R.C. BURRITO

1 fat-free 12-inch flour tortilla
2 heaping tablespoons
    fat-free shredded cheddar
    cheese

⅓ cup Spanish rice
    (recipe from page 160)
⅓ cup pinto beans
    (recipe from page 159)

See preparation directions on page 163.

Nutritional Facts (per serving)
    SERVING SIZE—1 BURRITO   TOTAL SERVINGS—1

	LITE	ORIGINAL
CALORIES	339	482
FAT	1G	15G

CLASSIC CHICKEN BURRITO

1 fat-free 12-inch flour tortilla
2 heaping tablespoons fat-free
  shredded cheddar cheese
1/3 cup Spanish rice
  (recipe from page 160)

1/3 cup pinto beans
  (recipe from page 159)
1/3 cup diced skinless chicken
  (recipe from page 157)

See preparation directions on page 163.

Nutritional Facts (per serving)
SERVING SIZE—1 BURRITO   TOTAL SERVINGS—1

	LITE	ORIGINAL
CALORIES	399	556
FAT	3G	22G

SPICY HOT CHICKEN BURRITO

1 fat-free 12-inch flour tortilla
2 heaping tablespoons
  fat-free shredded cheddar
  cheese
1/3 cup Spanish rice
  (recipe from page 160)

1/3 cup pinto beans
  (recipe from page 159)
1/3 cup diced skinless chicken
  (recipe from page 157)
1/2 tablespoon hot taco sauce
  (such as La Victoria brand)

See preparation directions on page 163.

Nutritional Facts (per serving)
SERVING SIZE—1 BURRITO   TOTAL SERVINGS—1

	LITE	ORIGINAL
CALORIES	402	559
FAT	3G	22G

LOCO GRANDE BURRITO

1 fat-free 12-inch flour tortilla
2 heaping tablespoons fat-free
   shredded cheddar cheese
⅓ cup Spanish rice
   (recipe from page 160)
⅓ cup pinto beans
   (recipe from page 159)

⅓ cup diced skinless chicken
   (recipe from page 157)
1 tablespoon guacamole
¼ cup chopped iceberg
   lettuce
¼ cup diced tomato
pinch chopped fresh cilantro

Nutritional Facts (per serving)
  SERVING SIZE—1 BURRITO   TOTAL SERVINGS—1

	LITE	ORIGINAL
CALORIES	434	632
FAT	5G	26G

1. Steam the tortilla in a steamer, or in a moist towel in the microwave for 20 seconds on high.
2. Build the burrito of your choice by arranging the ingredients across the center of a tortilla in the order listed. Leave room at each end for folding.
3. To fold, turn the left and right ends of the tortilla over the filling. Fold the bottom of the tortilla up over the ingredients, then continue rolling the burrito up into a tight package.

• EACH RECIPE SERVES 1.

• • • •

HOOTERS
BUFFALO CHICKEN WINGS

☆　✌　💣　✐　☯　✂　☞

You probably don't need me to tell you that traditional chicken wings have significant fat and calories. In most cases, the wings deep-fried in hot oil, the skin is left on the chicken, and then they are smothered in spicy sauce that is usually about half butter. So then, how can we possibly reduce the fat in a clone recipe for what has become one of the most popular chicken wings around without compromising the flavor and everything else that makes the Hooters version so addicting?

First of all, we must bake them instead of using the traditional frying method. As the wings bake, we'll keep the skin on at first, so that the meat will not dry out, then we'll ditch the stuff and replace it with spiced breading and a light coating of cooking spray. We'll bake the wings a bit more until they're golden brown, smother them with a fat-free spicy sauce, and *voilà!*—a Hooters Buffalo Chicken Wing clone that weighs in at around one-third the fat of the original version.

10 chicken wings with skin
¼ cup Crystal Louisiana Hot
　　Sauce or Frank's Red Hot
　　Cayenne Sauce
¼ cup Fleischmann's Fat-Free
　　Buttery Spread
1 tablespoon water

½ cup all-purpose flour
1 teaspoon salt
¼ teaspoon paprika
¼ teaspoon cayenne pepper
1 cup milk
canola oil nonstick spray

1. Preheat the oven on broil.
2. Line a cookie sheet or shallow baking pan with a sheet of aluminum foil. Spray the foil with nonstick spray.
3. Arrange the chicken wings on the foil with the side that has the most skin on it facing up. Broil the wings for 12 to 14 minutes, or until skin begins to dry.
4. Remove the wings from the oven, and set to 450 degrees. Allow the wings to cool for 10 to 15 minutes or just long enough so that they can be touched.
5. While the wings cool, prepare the sauce by combining the hot sauce, fat-free buttery spread, and water in a small saucepan over medium/low heat. Heat the mixture, stirring often, until it begins to boil. Immediately remove the sauce from the heat and cover the saucepan until the chicken wings are ready to coat.
6. Prepare the chicken breading by combining the flour with the salt, paprika, and cayenne pepper in a small bowl. Pour the milk into another small bowl.
7. When the wings are cool enough to touch, remove the skin from each of the chicken pieces, and discard it. Dip the wings, one at a time, in the breading, then into the milk and back in the breading, so that each one is well-coated.
8. Place the wings back on the baking sheet. Spray a coating of nonstick oil spray over each wing, so that the breading is moistened, and then bake the wings at 450 degrees for 12 minutes. Crank the oven up to broil for 3 to 5 minutes, or until the wings begin to brown and become crispy.
9. Remove the wings from the oven. Let them rest for about a minute, then put them into a plastic container (with a lid). Pour a generous amount of sauce over the wings, cover, and gently shake the wings so that they are all well coated with the sauce. Serve immediately.

- SERVES 2 AS AN APPETIZER.

Nutritional Facts *(per serving)*

SERVING SIZE—5 PIECES   TOTAL SERVINGS—2

	LITE	ORIGINAL
CALORIES (est.)	210	471
FAT (est.)	10G	30G

• • • •

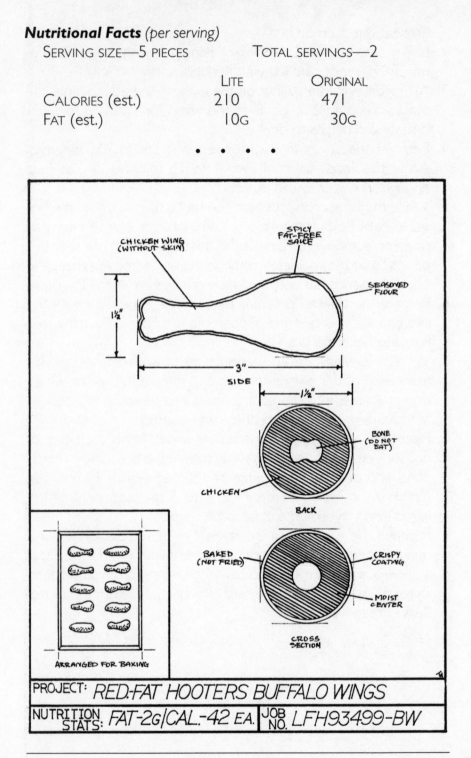

CHICKEN WING (WITHOUT SKIN)

SPICY FAT-FREE SAUCE

SEASONED FLOUR

1½"

3"

SIDE

1½"

BONE (DO NOT EAT)

CHICKEN

BACK

BAKED (NOT FRIED)

CRISPY COATING

MOIST CENTER

CROSS SECTION

ARRANGED FOR BAKING

PROJECT: *RED-FAT HOOTERS BUFFALO WINGS*

NUTRITION STATS: *FAT-2G/CAL.-42 EA.*   JOB NO. *LFH93499-BW*

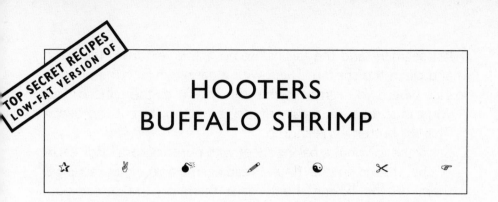

HOOTERS
BUFFALO SHRIMP

The Hooters chain continues its rapid expansion across the globe into 39 states and seven countries, including Taiwan, Aruba, Singapore, and Australia. In those 200 or so restaurants, this appetizer has become very popular since it was first introduced in 1995, as a variation on the Buffalo Chicken Wings recipe. Since this shrimp is fried, as are the chicken wings, we must resort to some tricks that will help bring the fat down. We'll bake the shrimp, rather than fry it, and prepare the sauce with a fat-free spread that adds flavor.

½ cup all-purpose flour
1 teaspoon salt
¼ teaspoon paprika
¼ teaspoon cayenne pepper
canola oil nonstick spray
12 large, uncooked (green)
    shrimp

¼ cup Crystal Louisiana Hot
    Sauce or Frank's Red Hot
    Cayenne Sauce
¼ cup Fleischmann's Fat-Free
    Buttery Spread
1 tablespoon water

1. Preheat the oven to 450 degrees.
2. Line a cookie sheet or shallow baking pan with a sheet of aluminum foil.
3. Make the breading by combining the flour, salt, paprika, and cayenne pepper in a small bowl.
4. Prepare the shrimp by cutting off the entire shell except the

last segment and the tailfins. Remove the vein from the back and clean the shrimp. Then, with a paring knife, cut a deeper slice where you removed the vein (down to the tail), so that you can spread the meat out. Be careful not to cut too deep. This will butterfly the shrimp.

5. Spray the foil on the baking sheet with nonstick spray. Roll each of the shrimp in the flour breading mixture. Then arrange them on the baking sheet. Place them on the spread-out, butterfly-cut, meaty part, with the tails sticking up. Spray each shrimp with a coating of nonstick spray, so that the breading is moistened.

6. Bake for 10 to 12 minutes or until the surface of the shrimp becomes light brown. Turn oven to broil for 4 to 5 minutes, or until the shrimp begin to brown and become crispy.

7. While the shrimp cooks, prepare the sauce by combining the hot sauce with the fat-free butter-flavored spread and a tablespoon of water in a small saucepan over medium/low heat. Cook it until the sauce starts to bubble, stirring occasionally, then reduce the heat to low and cover until the shrimp is ready.

8. When the shrimp is done, remove the pan from the oven, and let the shrimp sit for about a minute. Put all of the shrimp into a plastic container (with a lid), add a generous amount of the sauce, and cover. Gently shake the shrimp until each one is well coated with sauce. Pour the shrimp out onto a plate and serve hot.

- SERVES 2 AS AN APPETIZER.

Nutritional Facts (per serving)

SERVING SIZE—6 PIECES   TOTAL SERVINGS—2

	LITE	ORIGINAL
CALORIES (est.)	204	320
FAT (est.)	3G	10G

•　•　•　•

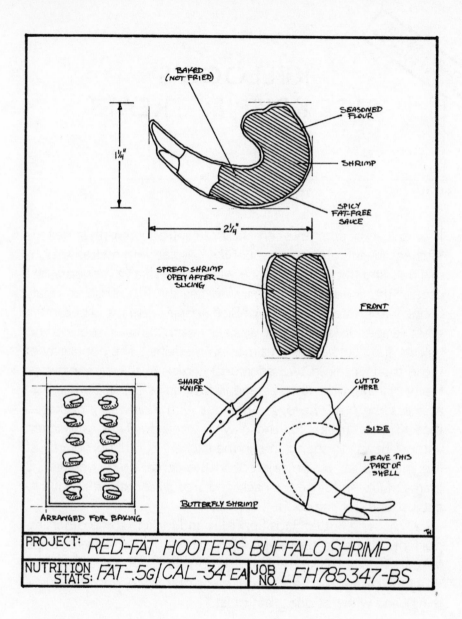

BAKED
(NOT FRIED)

SEASONED
FLOUR

SHRIMP

SPICY
FAT-FREE
SAUCE

1¼"

2¼"

SPREAD SHRIMP
OPEN AFTER
SLICING

FRONT

SHARP
KNIFE

CUT TO
HERE

SIDE

LEAVE THIS
PART OF
SHELL

BUTTERFLY SHRIMP

ARRANGED FOR BAKING

PROJECT: RED-FAT HOOTERS BUFFALO SHRIMP

NUTRITION
STATS: FAT-.5g/CAL-34 EA

JOB
NO. LFH785347-BS

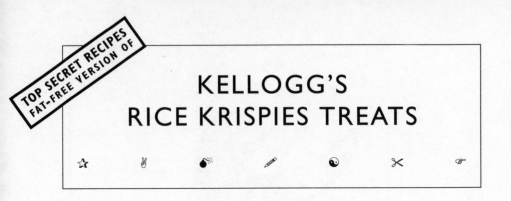

KELLOGG'S
RICE KRISPIES TREATS

It wasn't long after the cereal's 1928 introduction that Kellogg Kitchens invented a way to mix Rice Krispies with melted marshmallows and butter to produce with an alternative, nonbreakfast use for the product. In the early forties the Rice Krispies Treats recipe was printed on boxes of Rice Krispies cereal and became a great recipe for kids since it was very easy to make, required no baking, and could be eaten almost immediately. The popularity of these treats inspired two additional cereals in the early nineties: Fruity Marshmallow Krispies, and Rice Krispies Treats Cereal. And at the same time, Kellogg came out with individually packaged Rice Krispies Treats, for those who wanted instant satisfaction without having to spend time in the kitchen. But that product, just like the popular recipe printed on the cereal box, contained 2 grams of fat. And since the packaged Treats are small, it's tough to eat just one (tell me about it).

By using Butter Buds Sprinkles and making some other important changes to the recipe, I have come up with a treat recipe for bars that taste like the packaged product, at considerably less cost (the recipe makes the equivalent of three boxes of the real thing), and with not one gram of fat.

nonstick cooking spray
7 cups miniature marshmallows
3 tablespoons Butter Buds
   Sprinkles

2 tablespoons water
1/4 teaspoon vanilla
1/4 teaspoon salt
6 cups Rice Krispies cereal

1. Lightly coat a large nonstick saucepan or pot with cooking spray.
2. Add the marshmallows, Butter Buds, water, vanilla, and salt to the pan and set over medium/low heat. Stir the mixture constantly while cooking until the marshmallows are completely melted. Turn off the heat.
3. Add the Rice Krispies and stir until the cereal is completely coated.
4. Spray a 9 x 13-inch baking pan with a light coating of the cooking spray. Pour the Rice Krispies mixture into the pan. Moisten your hands and press the mixture into the pan until flat.
5. When the mixture cools completely, cut four times down and four across, making 25 bars.

- MAKES 25 BARS.

Nutritional Facts (per serving)

SERVING SIZE—1 BAR   TOTAL SERVINGS—25

	LITE	ORIGINAL
CALORIES	90	90
FAT	0G	2G

• • • •

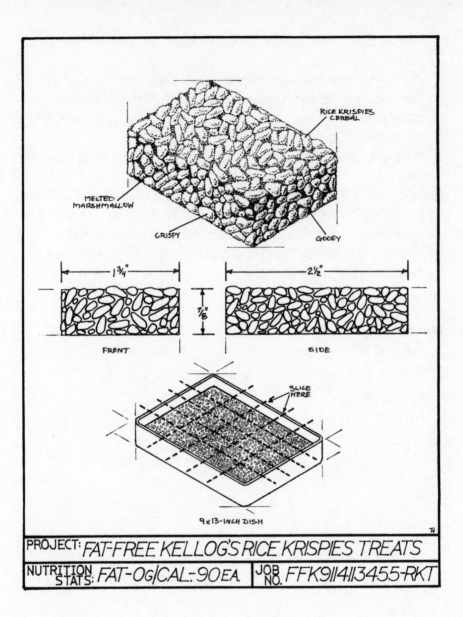

RICE KRISPIES
CEREAL

MELTED
MARSHMALLOW

CRISPY

GOOEY

1¾"

2½"

⅞"

FRONT

SIDE

SLICE
HERE

9x13-INCH DISH

TH

PROJECT: *FAT-FREE KELLOG'S RICE KRISPIES TREATS*

NUTRITION
STATS: *FAT-0G/CAL.-90EA.*

JOB
NO. *FFK911411345-RKT*

KFC
BUTTERMILK BISCUITS

How would you like a killer biscuit recipe that has 75 percent less fat than typical biscuits, and tastes great? And what if I told you they would still taste like those introduced to the world in 1982 by the world's largest chicken chain? Here you go—a clone recipe for making a low-fat version of KFC's Buttermilk Biscuits. Reduced-fat Bisquick and Butter Buds Sprinkles are the secret ingredients that help make this TSR low-fat conversion of a fast food favorite.

2 cups reduced-fat Bisquick
    baking mix
¾ cup low-fat (1 percent)
    buttermilk

2 teaspoons Butter Buds Sprinkles
2 teaspoons sugar
¼ teaspoon salt
1 tablespoon margarine, melted

1. Preheat the oven to 450 degrees.
2. Combine the baking mix, buttermilk, Butter Buds, sugar, and salt in a medium bowl. Mix by hand until well blended.
3. Turn the dough out onto a floured surface and knead for about 30 seconds, or until the dough becomes elastic.
4. Roll the dough to about ¾-inch thick and punch out biscuits using a 3-inch cutter. Arrange the punched-out dough on an ungreased baking sheet, and bake for 10 to 12 minutes or until the biscuits are golden on top and have about doubled in height.
5. Remove the biscuits from the oven and immediately brush the top of each one with a light coating of the melted margarine. Serve warm.

- MAKES 8 BISCUITS.

Nutritional Facts *(per serving)*
SERVING SIZE—1 BISCUIT   TOTAL SERVINGS—8

	LITE	ORIGINAL
CALORIES	115	180
FAT	2.5G	10G

• • • •

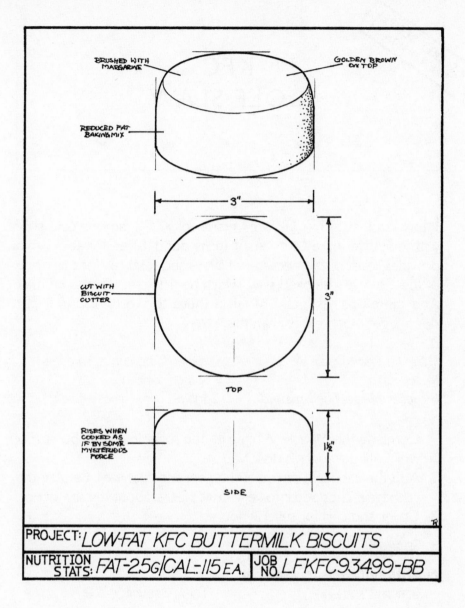

BRUSHED WITH
MARGARINE

GOLDEN BROWN
ON TOP

REDUCED FAT
BAKING MIX

3"

CUT WITH
BISCUIT
CUTTER

3"

TOP

RISES WHEN
COOKED AS
IF BY SOME
MYSTERIOUS
FORCE

1½"

SIDE

PROJECT: *LOW-FAT KFC BUTTERMILK BISCUITS*

NUTRITION STATS: *FAT-2.5g/CAL.-115 EA.*   JOB NO. *LFKFC93499-BB*

KFC
COLE SLAW

How cool is this? A fat-free version of KFC's famous cole slaw with only five ingredients! As it turns out, fat-free Miracle Whip provides most of the necessary flavors and textures for this clone of the Colonel's beloved slaw, which he first created in the fifties. And there's nary a gram of fat in there to worry about. It just doesn't get much easier than this.

1 cup fat-free Miracle Whip
1/4 cup sugar
8 cups cabbage, finely minced

2 tablespoons carrot, shredded
    then minced
2 tablespoons minced onion

1. Combine the Miracle Whip with the sugar in a large bowl. Mix well until the sugar is dissolved.
2. Add the cabbage, carrot, and onion, and toss well. Be sure the cabbage is chopped into very small pieces, about the size of rice.
3. Cover and chill for several hours.

- SERVES 8.

Nutritional Facts (per serving)
SERVING SIZE—   TOTAL SERVINGS—8
    APPROXIMATELY 3/4 CUP

	LITE	ORIGINAL
CALORIES	57	210
FAT	0G	10.5G

• • • •

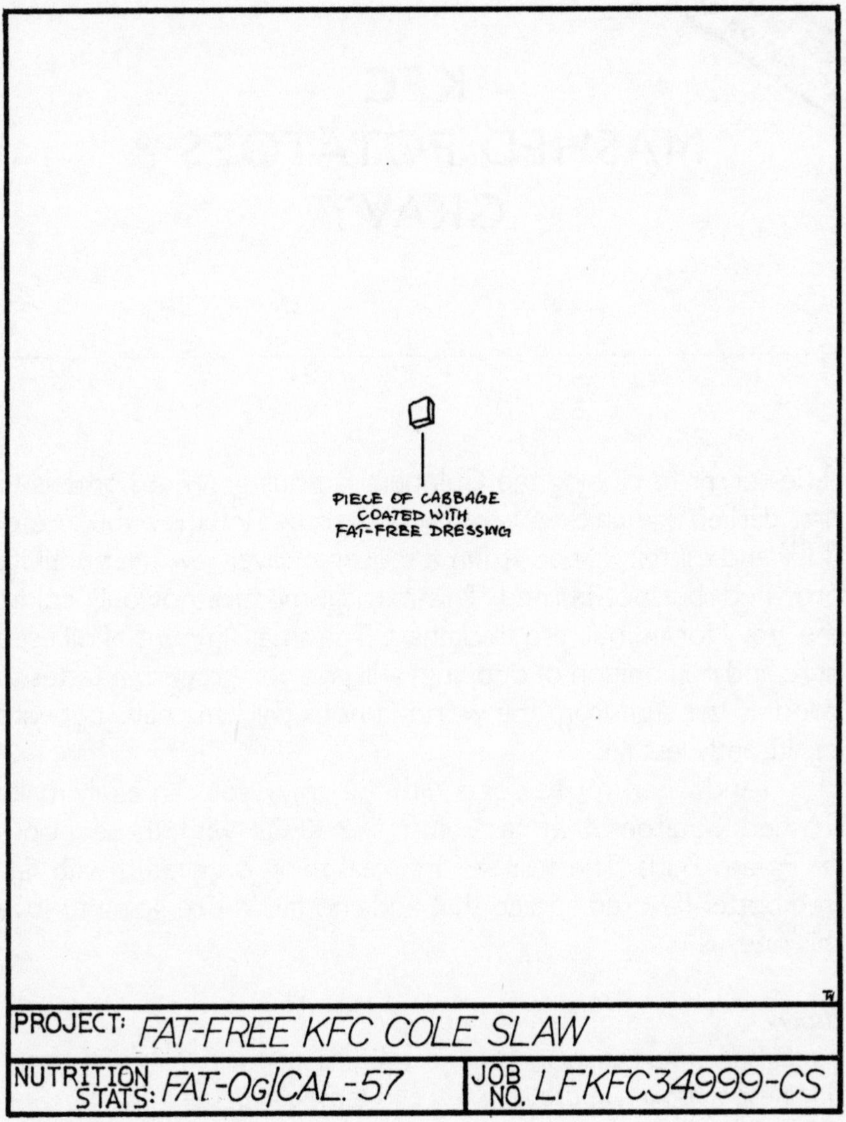

PIECE OF CABBAGE
COATED WITH
FAT-FREE DRESSING

PROJECT: FAT-FREE KFC COLE SLAW

NUTRITION STATS: FAT-0g/CAL.-57

JOB NO. LFKFC34999-CS

KFC
MASHED POTATOES &
GRAVY

The secret to cloning the Colonel's famous gravy at home is to first darken the chicken broth with a roux. Roux is a mixture of flour and oil that is cooked in a saucepan over low heat until it's browned, but not burned. This magical mixture not only colors the gravy for us, but also thickens it. The small amount of oil used here and no addition of drippings will give you gravy that tastes as good as the stuff from the world-famous chicken chain, but with significantly less fat.

And when you're done with the gravy, you can easily make mashed potatoes that taste just like KFC's with those popular Potato Buds. The taste of the real thing is imitated with fat-free butter-flavored spread that adds no fat. You're going to love this one.

GRAVY

1 tablespoon vegetable oil
5 tablespoons all-purpose flour
1 can Campbell's chicken broth
    (plus 1 can of water)

1/4 teaspoon salt
1/8 teaspoon pepper

MASHED POTATOES

1 1/2 cups water
1/3 cup reduced-fat (2 percent) milk
2 1/2 tablespoons Fleischmann's
    Fat-Free Buttery Spread

1/2 teaspoon salt
1 1/3 cups instant mashed potato
    flakes (Potato Buds)

1. Make the gravy by first preparing a roux: Combine the oil with 1½ tablespoons of flour in a medium saucepan. Cook over low heat for 20 to 30 minutes or until the mixture becomes a chocolate color.
2. Remove the pan from the heat and add the chicken broth, 1 can of water, the remaining flour, ¼ teaspoon of salt, and pepper. Put the pan back on the heat and bring the heat up to medium. When the mixture begins to boil, reduce the heat and simmer the gravy for 15 minutes or until thick.
3. As the gravy is reducing, prepare the potatoes by combining 1½ cups of water, ⅓ cup of milk, the fat-free buttery spread, and ½ teaspoon of salt in a medium saucepan over medium heat. Bring to a boil, add the potato flakes, and whip with a fork until smooth.
4. Serve the mashed potatoes with gravy poured over the top.

- MAKES 4 SERVINGS.

Nutritional Facts (per serving)
SERVING SIZE—½ CUP POTATOES   TOTAL SERVINGS—4
  AND 3 TABLESPOONS GRAVY

	LITE	ORIGINAL
CALORIES	120	120
FAT	2G	6G

• • • •

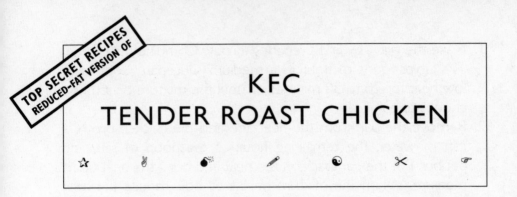

KFC
TENDER ROAST CHICKEN

Tender Roast chicken was introduced in 1996 after KFC axed Rotisserie Gold, its short-lived, whole-roasted chicken product that was meant to compete with home meal replacement chains like Boston Market and Kenny Rogers Roasters. Although it's not fried, as are the other KFC chicken offerings, six ounces of Tender Roast still has approximately 7.6 grams of fat when the skin is left on. That's why we're going to strip it all off. But not so fast, amigos. We'll keep that skin on through most of the baking process, so that the meat stays nice and juicy. Then, once the skin is peeled away, we can simply sprinkle the tasty spice blend over the juicy chicken and let it finish baking.

Serve this one with some of the other reduced-fat KFC clone recipes and you won't even miss the dozens of grams of fat you're avoiding.

SPICE BLEND
½ teaspoon salt
½ teaspoon pepper
½ teaspoon lemon pepper

¼ teaspoon thyme
¼ teaspoon paprika

1 whole roasting chicken, cut into
   pieces

1. Preheat the oven to 375 degrees.
2. Prepare the spice blend by combining the ingredients in a small bowl.
3. Place the chicken pieces onto a baking sheet, skin side up. Bake

for 20 minutes, then remove the chicken from the oven and cool for 5 to 10 minutes.

4. When you can handle the chicken, remove the skin, sprinkle the entire surface of the chicken with a light coating of the spice blend (approximately ½ teaspoon for a big piece, ¼ teaspoon for a small piece), and replace on the baking sheet. Return the sheet to the oven for 10 more minutes or until the chicken is done.

• SERVES 4.

Nutritional Facts (per serving)

SERVING SIZE—6 OUNCES   TOTAL SERVINGS—4

	LITE	ORIGINAL
CALORIES	206	338
FAT	7.6G	17.4G

• • • •

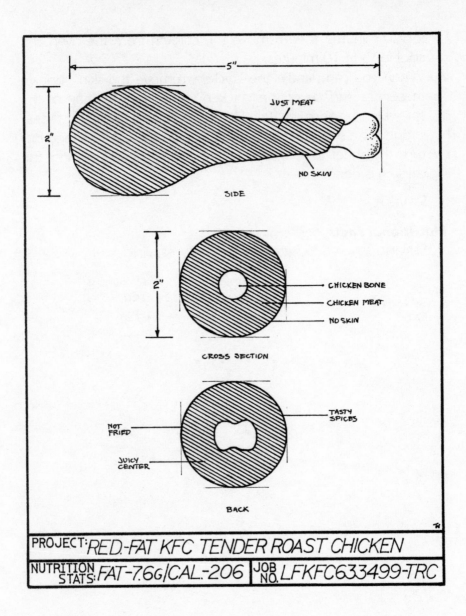

5"

2"

JUST MEAT

NO SKIN

SIDE

2"

CHICKEN BONE
CHICKEN MEAT
NO SKIN

CROSS SECTION

NOT FRIED

JUICY CENTER

TASTY SPICES

BACK

PROJECT: *RED.-FAT KFC TENDER ROAST CHICKEN*

NUTRITION STATS: *FAT-7.6G/CAL.-206* JOB NO. *LFKFC633499-TRC*

MCDONALD'S
BIG MAC

When the first Big Mac was served by a McDonald's franchisee in 1968, it was a time when all food in America was prepared with little attention to the amount of fat. Some low-calorie products had been developed, but they were not hugely popular, and most Americans ate and prepared food using whatever ingredients made it taste the best. Around 27 years later, McDonald's responded to the public's rapidly changing, health-conscious eating habits with the McLean Deluxe, a burger with a significantly reduced amount of fat. But the McLean Deluxe was not a commercial success; it never even came close to selling as fast as the other McDonald's burgers. Soon, the McLean Deluxe was history. And today, as reduced-fat products in supermarkets are selling faster than ever, McDonald's has not replaced the McLean Deluxe on its menu. The Big Mac is still king, with its 31 grams of fat. Here's a clone to make a version of the Big Mac at home with less than half the fat of the original.

FAT-FREE "SPECIAL SAUCE"

¼ cup fat-free mayonnaise
1 tablespoon fat-free French dressing
2 teaspoons sweet pickle relish
1 ½ teaspoons finely minced white
    onion

½ teaspoon white vinegar
½ teaspoon sugar
dash salt

2 sesame seed hamburger buns
2 additional top buns
½ pound super-lean ground beef
    (7 percent fat)
dash salt
dash pepper

2 teaspoons finely diced white
    onion
1 cup chopped lettuce
2 slices fat-free American
    cheese
dill pickle slices

1. Prepare the sauce by combining all of the sauce ingredients in a small bowl and mixing well. Cover and chill until needed.
2. With a serrated knife, cut the top (the rounded part) off both of the extra top buns. This will create two double-faced middle buns for your double-decker hamburgers. The part you cut off—the part with the sesame seeds—can be tossed.
3. Brown the faces of all the buns—including both sides of the two middle buns—in a frying pan or griddle that has been preheated to medium heat. Keep the pan hot.
4. Divide the meat into four ⅛-pound portions. Roll each one into a ball and press down onto wax paper to approximately the same diameter as the bun. Peel the beef patties from the wax paper and cook them in the hot pan or on the griddle. Lightly salt and pepper each patty and cook them for 2 to 3 minutes per side.
5. While the meat cooks, prepare the rest of the sandwich by spreading about a tablespoon of the sauce onto the face of the bottom bun, and the same amount onto the top face of the middle bun.
6. Sprinkle about ½ teaspoon of white onion onto the sauce on each of the four buns.
7. Divide the lettuce into four even portions and spread it on the onions on each of the sauce-covered buns.

8. Place a slice of American cheese on the lettuce on each of the two bottom buns.
9. Place two dill pickle slices on the lettuce on each of the two middle buns.
10. When the meat is done, place the patties on each of the bottom and middle buns on top of the other ingredients, then assemble the burger by stacking the middle buns onto the bottom buns, and finish it off with the top bun. Microwave the burger for 10 to 15 seconds, if you would like it to have that just-out-of-the-wrapper heat.

- SERVES 2.

Nutritional Facts *(per serving)*

SERVING SIZE—1 BURGER   TOTAL SERVINGS—2

	LITE	ORIGINAL
CALORIES	500	560
FAT	13G	31G

• • • •

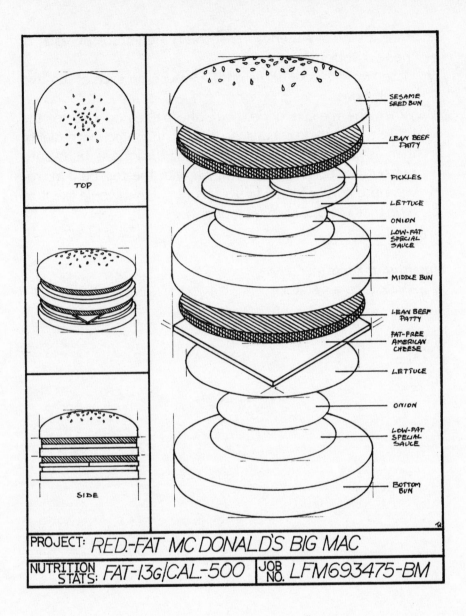

TOP

SIDE

SESAME
SEED BUN

LEAN BEEF
PATTY

PICKLES

LETTUCE

ONION

LOW-FAT
SPECIAL
SAUCE

MIDDLE BUN

LEAN BEEF
PATTY

FAT-FREE
AMERICAN
CHEESE

LETTUCE

ONION

LOW-FAT
SPECIAL
SAUCE

BOTTOM
BUN

PROJECT:	*RED.-FAT MC DONALD'S BIG MAC*
NUTRITION STATS: *FAT-13g/CAL.-500*	JOB NO. *LFM693475-BM*

MCDONALD'S BREAKFAST BURRITO

It was in the late seventies, shortly after McDonald's had introduced the Egg McMuffin, that the food giant realized the potential of a quick, drive-thru breakfast. Soon, the company had developed several breakfast selections, including the Big Breakfast with eggs, hash browns, and sausage. Eventually one out of every four breakfasts served out of the home would be served at McDonald's—an impressive statistic indeed. The newest kid on the McBreakfast block is this morning meal in a tortilla, first offered on the menu in the summer of 1991. The Breakfast Burrito has 19 grams of fat. To keep the energy up for your busy day, try out this version of the tasty breakfast meal with significantly reduced fat. Ay-yi-yi!

4 ounces turkey sausage
1 tablespoon minced white
  onion
½ tablespoon minced mild green
  chilies
1 cup egg substitute

salt
pepper
4 8-inch fat-free flour tortillas
4 slices fat-free American
  cheese

ON THE SIDE
salsa

1. Preheat a skillet over medium heat. Crumble the sausage into the pan, then add the onion. Sauté the sausage and onion for 3 to 4 minutes, or until the sausage is browned.
2. Add the mild green chilies and continue to sauté for 1 minute.
3. Pour the egg substitute into the pan and scramble the eggs with the sausage and vegetables. Salt and pepper to taste.
4. Heat up the tortillas by steaming them in the microwave in moist paper towels or a tortilla steamer for 20 to 30 seconds.
5. Break each slice of cheese in half and position two halves end-to-end in the middle of each tortilla.
6. To make the burrito, spoon ¼ of the egg filling onto the cheese in a tortilla. Fold one side of the tortilla over the filling, then fold up about two inches of one end. Fold over the other side of the tortilla to complete the burrito. Serve hot with salsa on the side, if desired.

- MAKES 4 BURRITOS.

Nutritional Facts (per serving)
SERVING SIZE—1 BURRITO   TOTAL SERVINGS—4

	LITE	ORIGINAL
CALORIES	202	320
FAT	2.5G	19G

• • • •

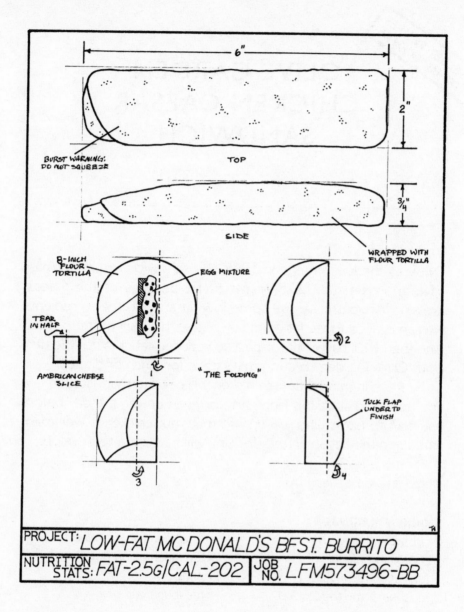

6"

2"

BURST WARNING:
DO NOT SQUEEZE

TOP

3/4"

SIDE

WRAPPED WITH
FLOUR TORTILLA

8-INCH
FLOUR
TORTILLA

EGG MIXTURE

TEAR
IN HALF

AMERICAN CHEESE
SLICE

"THE FOLDING"

2

3

TUCK FLAP
UNDER TO
FINISH

4

PROJECT: *LOW-FAT MC DONALD'S BFST. BURRITO*

NUTRITION STATS: *FAT-2.5G/CAL-202* **JOB NO.** *LFM573496-BB*

OLIVE GARDEN CHICKEN CAESAR SANDWICH

New to the lunch menu in 1995, this sandwich would normally have approximately 20.5 grams of fat because of the Caesar dressing. Ah, but if we use some low-fat and fat-free ingredients, we can reduce those fat grams by better than half of the original. And then we'll have a flavor-packed reduced-fat clone of the delicious Olive Garden creation that's great for lunch or dinner.

Keep in mind that the chicken will need to marinate for several hours, so start this one early, or even better, the day before you plan to eat it. This will ensure that your chicken is well marinated and the flavors in the dressing will have time to develop.

4 chicken breast fillets

CHICKEN MARINADE

I cup water	¼ teaspoon liquid smoke
I cup pineapple juice	¼ teaspoon onion powder
I tablespoon lime juice	¼ pepper
2 teaspoons soy sauce	⅛ teaspoon garlic
I teaspoon salt	

CAESAR DRESSING

¼ cup fat-free mayonnaise	I ½ teaspoons grated Parmesan cheese
I tablespoon egg substitute	⅛ teaspoon coarse-ground pepper
I teaspoon vinegar	

⅛ teaspoon garlic powder
⅛ teaspoon salt

dash onion powder
3 drops Worcestershire sauce

4 Italian or sourdough sandwich
   rolls

2 cups chopped romaine
   lettuce

1. Cut each chicken breast in half. Fold a piece of plastic wrap around one piece of chicken and pound flat (to about ¼-inch thick) with a mallet. The chicken should be slightly larger in diameter than the sandwich rolls. Repeat with the remaining pieces.
2. Combine the ingredients for the marinade in a medium bowl. Add the chicken, cover, and chill for at least 4 hours. Overnight is best.
3. While the chicken marinates, combine all of the Caesar dressing ingredients in a small bowl. Cover and chill.
4. When the chicken has marinated, preheat your barbecue or indoor grill to high heat. Grill the chicken for 2 to 3 minutes per side, or until done.
5. Use the grill to brown the faces of each roll.
6. Build each sandwich by spreading about a half cup of lettuce on one of the bottom buns. Drizzle about a tablespoon of the dressing over the lettuce. Next, stack two pieces of chicken on the sandwich. Place one piece of the chicken slightly off to one side and then position the second piece off to the other side but overlapping the first piece.
7. Finish off the sandwich with the top half of the roll. Repeat the process to build the remaining sandwiches and serve.

• SERVES 4.

Nutritional Facts (per serving)
   SERVING SIZE—1 SANDWICH   TOTAL SERVINGS—4

	LITE	ORIGINAL
CALORIES (est.)	450	543
FAT (est.)	9G	20.5G

• • • •

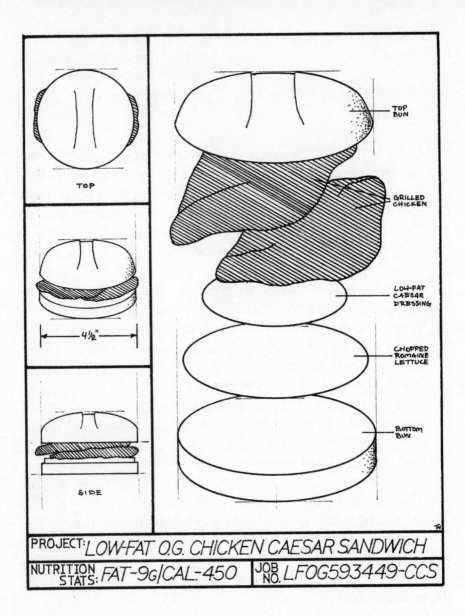

TOP

4½"

SIDE

TOP
BUN

GRILLED
CHICKEN

LOW-FAT
CAESAR
DRESSING

CHOPPED
ROMAINE
LETTUCE

BOTTOM
BUN

PROJECT: *LOW-FAT O.G. CHICKEN CAESAR SANDWICH*

NUTRITION STATS: *FAT-9G/CAL.-450*   **JOB NO.** *LFOG593449-CCS*

OLIVE GARDEN
ITALIAN SALAD DRESSING

We love to eat salad because it seems so healthy—all those veg-gies wrestling around in there. But add just a couple tablespoons of salad dressing and you've gone from zero fat to quite a lot of grams of the stuff, before your main course has even hit the table. And if the salad dressing is as tasty and addicting as the dressing the Olive Garden serves, you might be pouring on a lot more than just a couple tablespoons. So now we just have to figure out a way to cut those fat grams and hold on to the flavor of the dressing that has become so popular you can buy it by the bottle at the Olive Garden restaurants.

Let's do this: We'll take out the oil, and add dry pectin to thicken the dressing, along with more water than would be used in the original version. We can even put a good amount of Ro-mano cheese in there and still be sure that a single serving of the dressing has less than ½ gram of fat. Add some vinegar, a little corn syrup and lemon juice, some spices—bingo! Mission accom-plished. This one's a keeper.

⅔ cup water
1 ½ tablespoons dry pectin
½ cup white vinegar
¼ cup corn syrup
1 ¼ teaspoons salt
1 teaspoon lemon juice
½ teaspoon minced garlic
   (1 clove)

¼ teaspoon dried parsley
   flakes
pinch of dried oregano
pinch of crushed red pepper
   flakes
¼ cup egg substitute
2½ tablespoons grated Romano
   cheese

1. In a small saucepan, combine the water and dry pectin and whisk until the pectin is mostly dissolved.
2. Add the remaining ingredients, except for the Romano cheese, and place the pan over medium heat. Stir often until the mixture begins to boil, then remove the pan from the heat. Cool for about 10 minutes.
3. Stir the Romano cheese into the thickened mixture.
4. Allow the mixture to cool thoroughly, then pour it into a sealed container and chill for at least 2 hours.

- MAKES 1 ⅓ CUPS

Nutritional Facts *(per serving)*
SERVING SIZE—2 TABLESPOONS   TOTAL SERVINGS—11

	LITE	ORIGINAL
CALORIES	42	90
FAT	0G	8G

• • • •

OLIVE GARDEN
PASTA E FAGIOLI

☆   ✌   💣   ✎   ☯   ✂   ☞

One of the most popular and hard-to-pronounce items on the Olive Garden menu is found in the soup column. But it's more like a thick chili than a soup, really, with all those beans and veggies and ground beef in there. The reduced-fat grams in this clone are especially important when we consider that this dish makes an excellent meal by itself, and you may want to eat more than the 1 ½ cups serving size measured for the nutrition stats.

We'll keep the added fat to a minimum by sautéing the veggies in what little fat is not drained off from browning the super-lean ground beef. The soup will fill your mouth with so much flavor that it won't matter that we don't add any additional fat. You'll have a hard time distinguishing between this version and the original. Try it out, and you'll see what I mean.

This recipe makes about eight 1 ½-cup servings, so if you can't eat it all within a few days, it freezes well.

1 pound super-lean ground beef
   (7 percent fat)
1 small onion, diced (1 cup)
1 large carrot, julienned (1 cup)
3 stalks celery, chopped
   (1 cup)
2 cloves garlic, minced
2 14.5-ounce cans diced
   tomatoes
1 15-ounce can red kidney beans
   (with liquid)
1 15-ounce can great northern
   beans (with liquid)
1 15-ounce can tomato sauce
1 12-ounce can V-8 juice
1 tablespoon white vinegar
1½ teaspoons salt
1 teaspoon dried oregano
1 teaspoon dried basil
½ teaspoon pepper
½ teaspoon dried thyme
½ pound (½ package) ditali pasta

1. Brown the ground beef in a very large saucepan or soup pot over medium heat. Drain off the fat.
2. Add the onion, carrot, celery, and garlic and simmer for 10 minutes.
3. Add the remaining ingredients, except the pasta, and simmer for 1 hour.
4. About 50 minutes into the simmer time, cook pasta in 1½ to 2 quarts of boiling water over high heat. Cook for 10 minutes or just until pasta is *al dente*, or slightly tough. Drain.
5. Add the pasta to the large pot of soup. Simmer for 5 minutes and serve.

- SERVES 8 AS AN APPETIZER.

TIDBITS

Ditali pasta is small ¼-inch tubes of pasta—short, little hollow cylinders. They may also go by the name salad-roni.

Nutritional Facts (per serving)
SERVING SIZE—1½ CUPS   TOTAL SERVINGS—8

	LITE	ORIGINAL
CALORIES (est.)	312	416
FAT (est.)	4G	17.5G

• • • •

OLIVE GARDEN
TIRAMISU

You have now come to the most dramatic low-fat conversion recipe in this book, and one of the most unique. If you love tiramisu, but long for a lower-fat version, you should totally dig this one.

The Olive Garden chain offers a very popular and delicious tiramisu that is produced outside the restaurants and then delivered fresh to each outlet. The layers of fluffy mascarpone cheese and lady fingers soaked in a solution of strong coffee and coffee liqueur is a delicious and memorable combination. But mascarpone cheese has 13 grams of fat per ounce, and there's nothing that tastes quite like it.

However, there is one way to get very close; and it's a special combination of Dream Whip, gelatin, and fat-free cream cheese never before created and revealed in a cookbook. Entenmann's fat-free pound cake, sliced and brushed with a coffee/liqueur, will substitute nicely for the lady fingers. Layer it all into a square dish and you've got a "must try" TSR low-fat conversion clone that you won't forget.

FLUFFY CHEESE
1 cup low-fat milk (1 percent fat)
1 envelope unflavored gelatin
3 envelopes Dream Whip Mix

4 ounces Philadelphia fat-free
   cream cheese, softened
½ cup sugar

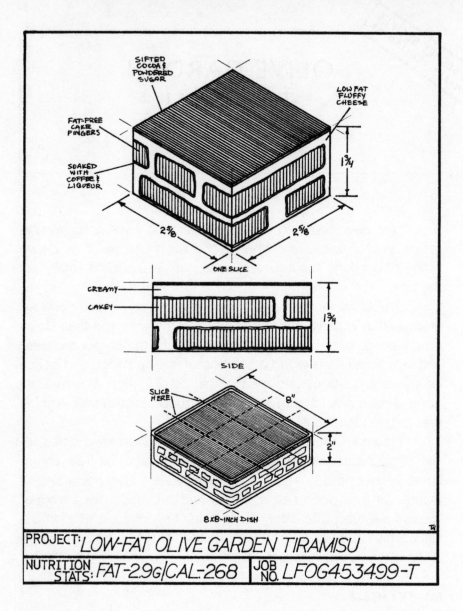

SIFTED COCOA & POWDERED SUGAR

LOW FAT FLUFFY CHEESE

FAT-FREE CAKE FINGERS

SOAKED WITH COFFEE & LIQUEUR

1¾

2⅝

2⅝

ONE SLICE

CREAMY

CAKEY

1¾

SIDE

SLICE HERE!

8"

2"

8 X 8-INCH DISH

PROJECT: *LOW-FAT OLIVE GARDEN TIRAMISU*

NUTRITION STATS: *FAT-2.9g/CAL-268* **JOB NO.** *LFOG453499-T*

CAKE

1 Entenmann's fat-free Golden Loaf, or use recipe on p. 49

1 tablespoon instant coffee

¼ cup plus 2 tablespoons hot water

1 tablespoon sugar

2 tablespoons Kahlua Coffee Liqueur

FOR TOP
cocoa powder

1. For the fluffy cheese, measure 1 cup of milk, remove 3 table-spoons, and set the rest aside. In a small bowl, combine the 3 tablespoons of milk with the gelatin. Let the mixture sit for 5 to 10 minutes, then microwave on half power for 2 minutes, or until the gelatin dissolves. Set this mixture aside to cool for 15 minutes.
2. Pour the remaining milk into a large mixing bowl. Add one envelope of Dream Whip at a time to the milk and beat after each addition for about 2 minutes until the mixture is light and fluffy.
3. In a separate bowl, beat together the softened cream cheese and the sugar. Add the gelatin/milk mixture and beat until smooth.
4. While beating the Dream Whip on high speed, add 1/3 of the cheese mixture at a time. Mix about 1 minute or until it is well-blended and smooth. Set aside while preparing the cake.
5. Cut the ends off the pound cake, then slice the remaining cake into 10 even slices. Discard the end pieces.
6. In a small bowl, mix the coffee with the hot water until the coffee dissolves. Add the sugar and stir until it dissolves as well. Add the Kahlua.
7. Cut each slice of cake into thirds (or in half, if using the recipe on p. 49), and arrange the slices on a wax paper–lined cookie sheet (rimmed to contain the liquid). Brush the coffee mixture generously over the top of each cake finger. Turn the fingers over and brush each once more with the coffee mixture.
8. To assemble the tiramisu, arrange the cake fingers side-by-side in an 8 x 8-inch baking dish. Leave about 1/4-inch between the cake fingers. Cover the fingers with half of the fluffy cheese mixture and spread carefully with a spatula until smooth and flat. Arrange the remaining cake fingers on the cheese mixture the same way as the first layers. Cover the cake with the remaining cheese mixture and smooth.
9. Put a couple teaspoons of cocoa powder into a sieve and tap it

over the top of the tiramisu to dust it with a light, even coating of the cocoa. Cover the tiramisu and chill it for at least 3 hours so that it sets up. When you're ready to serve, slice it into 9 even squares.

• SERVES 9.

Nutritional Facts *(per serving)*
SERVING SIZE—1 SLICE   TOTAL SERVINGS—9 SLICES

	LITE	ORIGINAL
CALORIES (est.)	268	475
FAT (est.)	2.9G	38G

• • • •

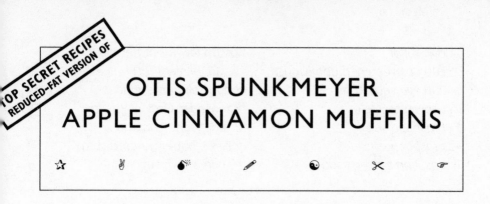

OTIS SPUNKMEYER
APPLE CINNAMON MUFFINS

So who is this Otis Spunkmeyer guy, anyway? Actually, it's no one at all. The character who flies around in the plane that's pictured on the product labels, searching the world for premium ingredients for his line of baked goods, is just a catchy name dreamed up by founder Ken Rawlings's 12-year-old daughter.

The company offers low-fat versions of many of its 11 varieties of muffins, but they are more difficult to track down than the original versions. So we've got a clone here that uses some tricks to replace a lot of the fat.

While this reduced-fat conversion clone recipe of the famous Texas-size muffins has 4 grams of fat per serving, or 8 grams total, it's still quite a saving compared to the original muffins, which have a total of 22 grams of fat each.

¾ cup sugar
⅔ cup unsweetened applesauce
¼ cup egg substitute
¼ cup vegetable oil
¾ teaspoon salt
½ teaspoon vanilla
1 teaspoon baking soda

½ cup low-fat buttermilk
 (1 percent fat)
2 cups all-purpose flour
2 teaspoons baking powder
2 teaspoons cinnamon
fat-free butter-flavored spray
⅓ cup brown sugar

1. Preheat the oven to 325 degrees.
2. In a large bowl, mix together the sugar, applesauce, egg substitute, oil, salt, vanilla, and baking soda. Add the buttermilk and blend.
3. In a separate bowl sift together the flour, baking powder, and cinnamon. Add the dry ingredients to the wet, and mix well with an electric mixer.
4. To bake the muffins, use a "Texas-size" muffin pan lined with large muffin cups. You may also bake the muffins without the cups, just be sure to grease the cups well with cooking spray. (If you use a regular-size muffin pan, which also works fine, your cooking time will be a few minutes less and your yield will double.) Fill the cups halfway with batter.
5. Spray a couple of squirts of fat-free butter-flavored spray over the top of each cup of batter. Follow that with a sprinkle of about 1 teaspoon of brown sugar.
6. Bake the muffins for 20 to 24 minutes or until brown on top (16 to 20 minutes for regular-size muffins). Remove the muffins from the oven and allow them to cool for about 30 minutes. Then put the muffins in a sealed container or resealable plastic bag.

• MAKES 8 TEXAS-SIZE MUFFINS (OR 16 REGULAR-SIZE MUFFINS).

Nutritional Facts (per serving)
SERVING SIZE—½ MUFFIN   TOTAL SERVINGS—16

	LITE	ORIGINAL
CALORIES	142	220
FAT	4G	11G

• • • •

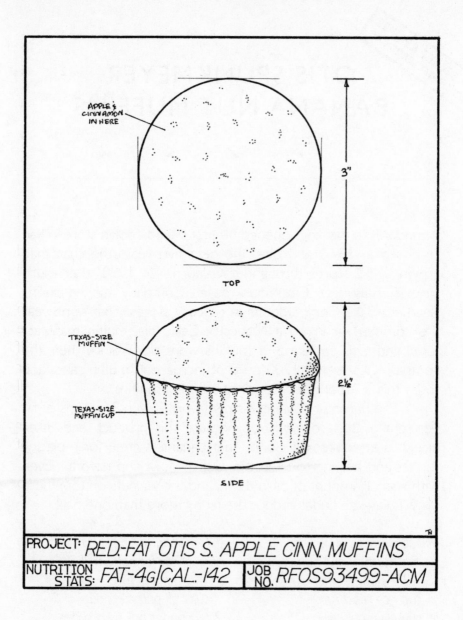

APPLE &
CINNAMON
IN HERE

3"

TOP

TEXAS-SIZE
MUFFIN

TEXAS-SIZE
MUFFIN CUP

2½"

SIDE

PROJECT: *RED-FAT OTIS S. APPLE CINN. MUFFINS*

NUTRITION STATS: *FAT-4g/CAL.-142*   JOB NO. *RFOS93499-ACM*

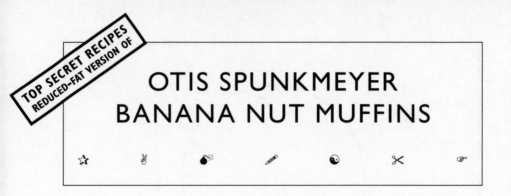

OTIS SPUNKMEYER
BANANA NUT MUFFINS

Founder Ken Rawlings opened his first baked cookie store in San Francisco in 1977, and over the next five years the chain had grown to 22 stores throughout California. In 1990, after much success, Rawlings's Otis Spunkmeyer Company started selling Ready-to-Bake Cookie dough in grocery stores. That same year the company acquired a Modesto, California, muffin manufacturer, and Otis Spunkmeyer Muffins were born. Since then, the company has seen a 1200 percent increase in muffin sales, and today this is America's best-selling brand of muffins.

The banana-nut variety is my favorite, with 24 grams of fat per muffin. But we're in luck, because this product lends itself nicely to a reduced-fat clone. That banana is great for replacing the fat and helping to keep the muffin moist and flavorful. Even with a small amount of oil in there, and the walnuts on top, these tasty Texas-size dudes reduce the fat by more than one-half.

¾ cup sugar
⅔ cup mashed ripe banana
   (2 medium bananas)
¼ cup egg substitute
¼ cup vegetable oil
¾ teaspoon salt
½ teaspoon vanilla
¼ teaspoon banana extract

1 teaspoon baking soda
½ cup low-fat buttermilk
   (1 percent fat)
2 cups all-purpose flour
2 teaspoons baking powder
fat-free butter-flavored spray
¼ cup chopped walnuts

1. Preheat the oven to 325 degrees.
2. In a large bowl, mix together the sugar, mashed banana, egg substitute, oil, salt, vanilla, banana extract, and baking soda. Add the buttermilk and blend well.
3. In a separate bowl sift together the flour and baking powder. Add the dry ingredients to the wet and mix well with an electric mixer.
4. To bake the muffins, use a "Texas-size" muffin pan lined with large muffin cups. You may also bake the muffins without the cups, just be sure to grease the cups well with cooking spray. (If you use a regular size muffin pan, which also works fine, your cooking time will be a few minutes less and your yield will double.) Fill the cups halfway with batter.
5. Spray a couple of squirts of fat-free butter-flavored spray over the top of each cup of batter. Follow that with a sprinkle of about ½ tablespoon of chopped walnuts.
6. Bake the muffins for 20 to 24 minutes or until brown on top (16 to 20 minutes for regular-size muffins). Remove the muffins from the oven and allow them to cool for about 30 minutes. Then put the muffins in a sealed container or resealable plastic bag.

• MAKES 8 TEXAS-SIZE MUFFINS (OR 16 REGULAR-SIZE MUFFINS).

Nutritional Facts (per serving)

SERVING SIZE—½ MUFFIN   TOTAL SERVINGS—16

	LITE	ORIGINAL
CALORIES	147	240
FAT	5G	12G

• • • •

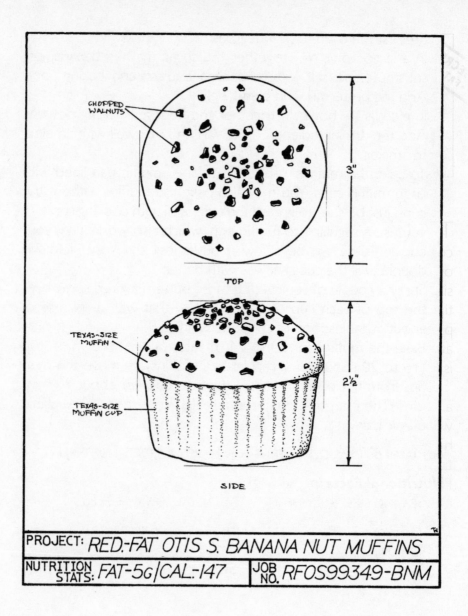

CHOPPED
WALNUTS

3"

TOP

TEXAS-SIZE
MUFFIN

TEXAS-SIZE
MUFFIN CUP

2½"

SIDE

PROJECT: *RED.-FAT OTIS S. BANANA NUT MUFFINS*

NUTRITION STATS: *FAT-5G/CAL.-147*

JOB NO. *RFOS99349-BNM*

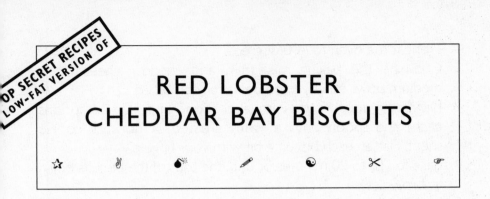

RED LOBSTER
CHEDDAR BAY BISCUITS

The cheesy little biscuits that come with your meal at the country's largest seafood chain were first served in 1990 as a part of each entrée. According to a company spokesperson, it's the single item that the chain has now become best known for. It's estimated that in 1997 the chain served over 435 million of these puppies. And since it's the most requested recipe on the Internet and on the *topsecretrecipes.com* Web site, I figure it's time to satisfy those requests.

But, since this is a book of low-fat and reduced-fat recipes, and since each of those small biscuits has around 7 grams of fat, we're going to make this recipe unique. I'm going to show you how to make a delicious light version of this popular treat which tastes just as good as the original. The key is using reduced-fat Bisquick, as well as reduced-fat shredded cheddar cheese. This is an easy recipe to make, and these biscuits are scrumptious.

2 cups reduced-fat Bisquick
    baking mix
¾ cup low-fat buttermilk
    (1 percent fat)
1 cup reduced-fat shredded
    cheddar cheese

2 tablespoons Fleischmann's
    Fat-Free Buttery Spread
¼ teaspoon garlic powder
¼ teaspoon dried parsley flakes,
    crushed fine

1. Preheat the oven to 400 degrees.
2. Combine the baking mix, milk, and cheddar cheese in a medium bowl. Mix by hand until well combined.
3. Divide the dough into 12 equal portions (about 3 tablespoons each) and spoon onto a lightly greased or nonstick cookie sheet. Flatten each biscuit a bit with your fingers.
4. Bake for 18 to 20 minutes or until the tops of the biscuits begin to brown.
5. In a small bowl, combine the buttery spread with the garlic powder. Heat this mixture for 30 seconds in the microwave, then brush a light coating over the top of each biscuit immediately after removing them from the oven. Sprinkle a dash of parsley over the top of each biscuit.

- MAKES 12 BISCUITS

TIDBITS

To make fine parsley flakes, as can be found on the original, simply crush the flakes between your thumb and forefinger.

Nutritional Facts (per serving)

SERVING SIZE—1 BISCUIT   TOTAL SERVINGS—12

	LITE	ORIGINAL
CALORIES (est.)	112	130
FAT (est.)	3G	7G

• • • •

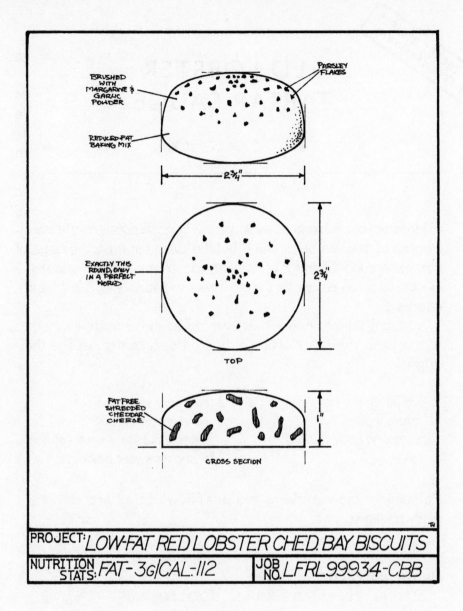

BRUSHED
WITH
MARGARINE &
GARLIC
POWDER

PARSLEY
FLAKES

REDUCED-FAT
BAKING MIX

2¾"

EXACTLY THIS
ROUND, ONLY
IN A PERFECT
WORLD

2¾"

TOP

FAT FREE
SHREDDED
CHEDDAR
CHEESE

1"

CROSS SECTION

PROJECT: *LOW-FAT RED LOBSTER CHED. BAY BISCUITS*

NUTRITION STATS: *FAT-3g/CAL-112*

JOB NO. *LFRL99934-CBB*

RED LOBSTER
TARTAR SAUCE

Alongside your fish entrée served at this huge seafood chain, comes a dollop of delicious tartar sauce. But the sauce served at the restaurant has around 22 grams of fat per two tablespoons. This adds significant fat to an entrée that is otherwise so naturally light in fat and calories.

Using fat-free mayonnaise, we can easily eliminate every bit of the fat in this sauce. The finished product tastes just like the original.

½ cup fat-free
   mayonnaise
1 tablespoon finely minced
   onion

2 teaspoons shredded
   and chopped carrot
   (bits should be the size of rice)
2 teaspoons sweet pickle relish

Combine all the ingredients in a small bowl. Cover and chill until ready to serve.

• MAKES ½ CUP.

Nutritional Facts (per serving)
  SERVING SIZE—2 TABLESPOONS   TOTAL SERVINGS—4

	LITE	ORIGINAL
CALORIES (est.)	25	200
FAT (est.)	0G	22G

• • • •

SHONEY'S
HOT FUDGE CAKE

☆ ✌ 💣 ✏ ☯ ✂ ☞

If you've ever laid your fork into one of these babies, you know how tough it is to take only a bite or two. Now you don't have to stop just as it's getting good. TSR drastically reduces the fat in this clone of the Shoney's creation with the help of reduced-fat devil's food cake mix and fat-free ice cream. Just be sure to get the type of ice cream that comes in a rectangular container, so that slicing and arranging the ice cream on the cake is made easier. Breyer's makes excellent fat-free vanilla ice cream and the container works well for this recipe. You may have some ice cream left over, which you can then eat with the small cake or cupcakes you can bake with the cup of leftover cake batter.

1 18.25-ounce box reduced-fat devil's food cake mix	1 half-gallon box fat-free ice cream (Breyer's is good)
1 ⅓ cups water	1 16-ounce jar chocolate fudge topping
2 tablespoons vegetable oil	1 can whipped cream
¾ cup egg substitute	12 maraschino cherries

1. Preheat the oven to 350 degrees.
2. Mix the batter for the cake as instructed on the box of the cake mix by combining the mix with the water, oil, and eggs in a large mixing bowl.
3. Remove a scant 1 cup of the batter from the bowl and set it aside, then add the remaining batter to a well-greased 9 × 13-inch baking pan. We won't be using the extra batter that

was set aside, so you can discard it or use it for another recipe, such as cupcakes.

4. Bake the cake according to the box instructions (about 30 minutes). Allow the cake to cool completely.

5. When the cake has cooled, carefully remove it from the pan and place it right side up onto a sheet of wax paper. With a long knife (a bread knife works great) slice the cake horizontally through the middle, and carefully remove the top. It helps to position the cake near the edge of your kitchen counter so that you can get a straight cut through the middle of the cake.

6. Pick up the wax paper with the bottom half of the cake still on it, and place it back into the baking pan.

7. Take the ice cream from the freezer and, working quickly, tear or cut the box open so that you can slice the ice cream like bread.

8. Make six ¾-inch slices of ice cream and arrange them side-by-side on the cake in the pan. Cover the entire surface of the cake with the ice cream slices. Fill in any gaps with additional ice cream. You may have about one-fifth of the ice cream left over in the box.

9. When you have covered the entire surface of the bottom cake half with ice cream slices, carefully place the top half of the cake, right side up, onto the ice cream in the pan. You should now have a layer of fat-free ice cream sandwiched between the two halves of reduced-fat cake. Cover the entire pan with plastic wrap or foil (trim the wax paper from the edges if necessary), and place the pan into your freezer for at least a couple of hours.

10. When you are ready to serve the dessert, slice the cake so that it will make 12 equal slices—that is, cut lengthwise twice and crosswise three times. If you will not be serving the entire desert, only slice what you will be using and save the rest, covered, in the freezer until you are ready to use it (it should keep for several weeks).

11. Heat up the fudge in the microwave or in a jar immersed in a saucepan of water over medium/low heat.

12. Pour about 2 tablespoons of fudge over the top of each slice of cake, and then add a small portion of whipped cream (about 2 tablespoons) on top of that.
13. Place a cherry onto the pile of whipped cream and serve immediately.

• SERVES 12.

Nutritional Facts *(per serving)*

SERVING SIZE—1 SLICE   TOTAL SERVINGS—12

	LITE	ORIGINAL
CALORIES	328	522
FAT	9.5G	20G

• • • •

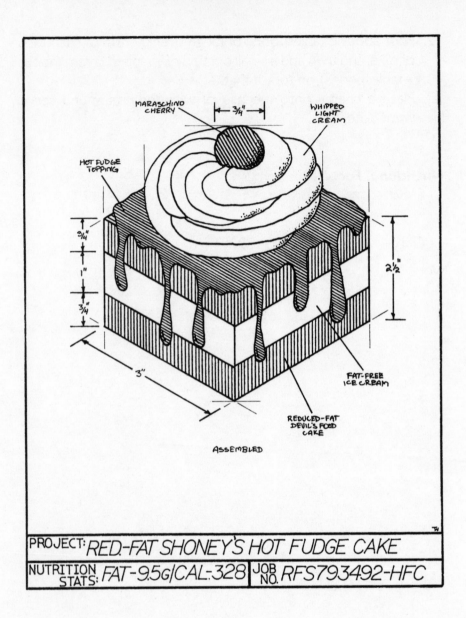

MARASCHINO CHERRY

WHIPPED LIGHT CREAM

HOT FUDGE TOPPING

3/4"

3/4"

1"

3/4"

2½"

3"

FAT-FREE ICE CREAM

REDUCED-FAT DEVIL'S FOOD CAKE

ASSEMBLED

TH

PROJECT:	*RED.-FAT SHONEY'S HOT FUDGE CAKE*
NUTRITION STATS:	*FAT-9.5g/CAL-328*	JOB NO.	*RFS793492-HFC*

214

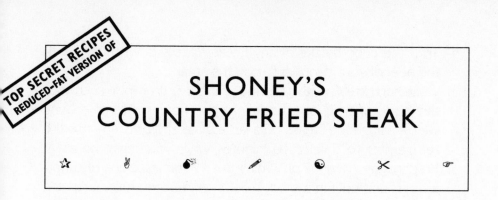

SHONEY'S
COUNTRY FRIED STEAK

Okay, you got me. This TSR version of one of Shoney's most popular country-style items is not really fried. If it were, it surely wouldn't have nearly one-fourth the fat of the original, which you can order at any of the 900 restaurants that make up this mostly Southern U.S. chain. But you'll swear this version tastes like the original, because we still bread the steak, and then spray it with a light coating of cooking spray. Once it's baked, then broiled to a golden brown, the steak is smothered with very low-fat gravy. Check out how these low-fat cooking tricks used here make a country steak that's just as good as the fried version.

1 cup all-purpose flour
½ tablespoon salt
⅛ teaspoon pepper

1 cup fat-free milk
4 4-ounce cube steaks

LOW-FAT COUNTRY GRAVY
1½ tablespoons super-lean
   ground beef (7 percent fat)
heaping ⅓ cup all-purpose flour
2 cups fat-free chicken stock

2 cups fat-free milk
½ teaspoon salt
¼ teaspoon pepper

vegetable oil cooking spray

1. Preheat the oven to 425 degrees.
2. Combine the flour, salt, and pepper in a large shallow bowl.
3. Pour the milk into another shallow bowl.

4. Trim the cube steaks of any fat and press down firmly with the heel of your hand to flatten the steaks.
5. Coat each steak with the flour mixture, then put each into the bowl of milk, and back into the flour mixture, coating well. Arrange the steaks on a large plate and pop 'em into the refrigerator to chill for 10 minutes, while you begin the gravy.
6. Prepare the gravy by browning the 1½ tablespoons of super-lean ground beef in a small skillet over medium heat. Crumble the meat into tiny pieces as you cook it.
7. Transfer the browned meat into a medium saucepan. Add ¼ cup of flour to the pan and stir it in with the meat. Add the remaining ingredients for the gravy except the cooking spray, whisk to combine, turn the heat to high, and bring the mixture to a boil, stirring often. Reduce the heat and simmer the mixture for 15 to 20 minutes until thick. Turn the heat to low to keep the gravy hot as the steaks are prepared.
8. Spray a cooking sheet generously with the cooking spray and arrange the floured steaks side-by-side on the cooking sheet. Spray the top surface of the meat with a coating of the cooking spray and place the steaks into the oven to bake for 5 to 7 minutes.
9. Crank the oven up to broil and cook the steaks for 7 minutes, flip each one over, then broil for an additional 5 to 7 minutes or until the surface of the steaks is browned.
10. Serve the steaks with gravy poured over the top, with a side of mashed potatoes, grits, or steamed vegetables, if desired.

Nutritional Facts (per serving)

SERVING SIZE—1 STEAK   TOTAL SERVINGS—4

	LITE	ORIGINAL
CALORIES	260	563
FAT	10G	37G

• • • •

TACO BELL
BEEF SOFT TACO

*Y*o *quiero* low-fat Taco Bell? Apparently not when faced with a choice. It took only one year for Taco Bell execs to cut the eight-item Border Lights selection from the Taco Bell menu in 1996. Those items, which featured several different taco and burrito selections, were made with reduced-fat ingredients. But, as other fast food companies discovered with their own discontinued light products, customers who roll into the drive-thrus aren't interested lower fat offerings. That is their time of the week to bite into something filled with flavor and just enjoy.

On the other hand, when we cook at home, and want to clone the flavor of food like that served at Taco Bell, it takes no extra effort to make the meal significantly lower in fat. So why not give this delicious recipe a go? And you'll soon find out these tacos will taste just like the soft tacos you get from the world's largest Mexican food chain, but with only one-quarter of the fat.

½ pound super-lean ground beef
    (7 percent fat)
2 tablespoons all-purpose flour
¾ teaspoon salt
¼ teaspoon dried minced onion
¼ teaspoon paprika
1 ½ teaspoons chili powder
dash garlic powder

dash onion powder
¼ cup water
5 6-inch fat-free flour tortillas
½ cup plus 2 tablespoons
    shredded iceberg lettuce
5 tablespoons fat-free shredded
    cheddar cheese

1. In a medium bowl combine the super-lean ground beef with the flour, salt, minced onion, paprika, chili powder, garlic powder, and onion powder. Use your hands to thoroughly incorporate everything into the ground beef.
2. Preheat a skillet over medium/low heat and add the ground beef mixture to the pan along with the water. Brown the beef mixture for 5 to 6 minutes, using a wooden spoon or spatula to break up the beef as it cooks.
3. Using the microwave, heat up the fat-free flour tortillas wrapped in a moist cloth or paper towels, or use a tortilla steamer. Heat for 25 to 30 seconds, or until hot.
4. Spoon about 3 tablespoons of the beef mixture into the center of one tortilla.
5. Place about 2 tablespoons of shredded lettuce on top of the beef.
6. Finish the soft taco by spreading about a tablespoon of shredded cheese over the lettuce and fold. Repeat for the remaining tacos.

- MAKES 5 SOFT TACOS.

Nutritional Facts *(per serving)*
SERVING SIZE—1 TACO   TOTAL SERVINGS—5

	LITE	ORIGINAL
CALORIES	170	225
FAT	3G	12G

• • • •

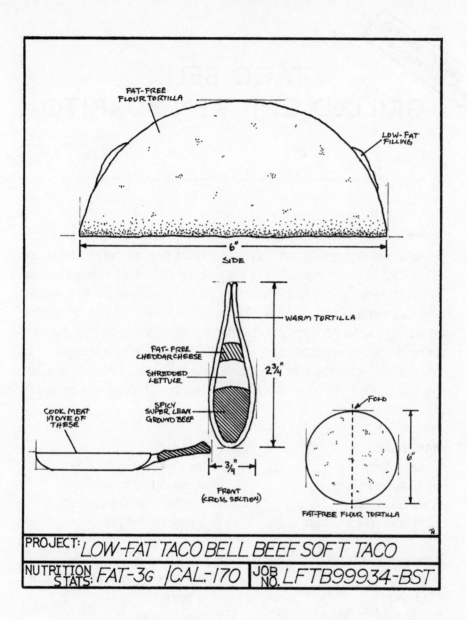

FAT-FREE
FLOUR TORTILLA

LOW-FAT
FILLING

6"
SIDE

WARM TORTILLA

FAT-FREE
CHEDDAR CHEESE

SHREDDED
LETTUCE

SPICY
SUPER LEAN
GROUND BEEF

2¾"

COOK MEAT
IN ONE OF
THESE

3/4"

FRONT
(CROSS SECTION)

FOLD

6"

FAT-FREE FLOUR TORTILLA

PROJECT: *LOW-FAT TACO BELL BEEF SOFT TACO*

NUTRITION STATS: *FAT-3g | CAL.-170*   JOB NO. *LFTB99934-BST*

TACO BELL
GRILLED CHICKEN BURRITO

☆   ✌   💣   ✒   ☯   ✂   ☞

When Glen Bell opened the first Taco Bell in 1962, he probably never envisioned that one day he would see his name on more than 10,000 locations serving his special brand of Americanized Mexican fast food. He probably also didn't expect there would one day be a book that would show you how to get significant fat savings when creating a low-fat kitchen clone of this popular menu item—around 80 percent less fat than the real thing!

You'll want to start this one several hours before, or even the day before you plan to eat it, so that the chicken can properly marinate.

MARINADE

½ cup water

1 teaspoon soy sauce

1 teaspoon salt

1 teaspoon brown sugar

½ teaspoon onion powder

¼ teaspoon liquid smoke

¼ teaspoon black pepper

¼ teaspoon chili powder

2 chicken breast fillets

1 cup instant rice

1 cup water

½ cup mild enchilada sauce

½ teaspoon salt

4 12-inch fat-free flour tortillas

⅓ cup fat-free shredded cheddar cheese

⅓ cup reduced-fat shredded Monterey Jack cheese

1. In a small bowl combine the ½ cup water, soy sauce, salt, brown sugar, onion powder, liquid smoke, black pepper, and chili powder. Pour the mixture over the chicken breasts and

marinate overnight. You can marinate for less time if you wish, but overnight is much better.

2. Cook the chicken on your barbecue or indoor grill over medium/high heat for 5 to 6 minutes per side, or until done. Slice the chicken into bite-size chunks.

3. While the chicken cooks, prepare the rice following the instructions on the box. It will probably tell you to bring the water to a boil, then add the rice, stir, cover, remove from the heat, and let it sit for 5 minutes.

4. When the rice is cooked, add the enchilada sauce and salt to the saucepan. Put the rice over low heat, uncovered, and cook until hot.

5. Heat the tortillas in a steamer, or wrap them in moist towels and heat on high for 25 to 30 seconds in the microwave.

6. Build a burrito by spreading ¼ of the chicken down the middle of one of the tortillas. Leave room at the ends for folding.

7. Spread ⅓ cup of rice over the chicken.

8. Sprinkle a heaping tablespoon of each of the cheeses over the rice.

9. Fold the left side of the tortilla over the filling, then fold up the bottom of the tortilla. Finish the burrito by folding the right side over and serve hot. Repeat for the remaining burritos. You may want to heat up each burrito in the microwave for 20 to 30 seconds to help the cheeses melt.

- MAKES 4 BURRITOS.

Nutritional Facts (per serving)

SERVING SIZE—1 BURRITO   TOTAL SERVINGS—4

	LITE	ORIGINAL
CALORIES	157	400
FAT	5G	16G

• • • •

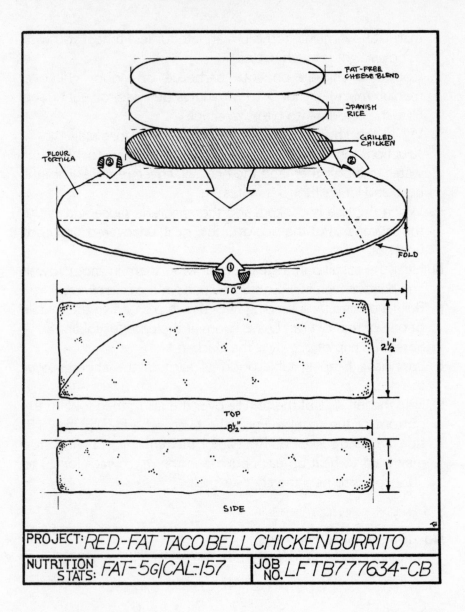

FAT-FREE
CHEESE BLEND

SPANISH
RICE

GRILLED
CHICKEN

FLOUR
TORTILLA

③

②

FOLD

①

10"

2½"

TOP

8½"

1"

SIDE

PROJECT: *RED.-FAT TACO BELL CHICKEN BURRITO*

NUTRITION STATS: *FAT-5g/CAL:157*

JOB NO. *LFTB777634-CB*

TACO BELL
MEXICAN PIZZA

You probably didn't realize that these delicious pizzas you get from the world's largest Mexican food chain have 36 grams of fat. But they are good, and if you like 'em as much as I do, you'll be happy to know that you can make a version of your own at home with only 10 grams of fat.

The secret fat savings come from baking, rather than frying, the flour tortillas. You'll also adios much of the fat by using reduced-fat cheddar and jack cheeses. I picked reduced-fat for these, because the fat-free stuff does not melt well in the final baking step for the finished pizza.

½ pound super-lean ground beef
    (7 percent fat)
2 tablespoons all-purpose flour
¾ teaspoon salt
¼ teaspoon dried minced onion
¼ teaspoon paprika
1 ½ teaspoons chili powder
dash garlic powder
dash onion powder
¼ cup water
8 6-inch fat-free flour tortillas

vegetable oil nonstick cooking
    spray
1 ⅓ cups fat-free refried beans
⅔ cup mild Picante salsa
½ cup reduced-fat shredded
    cheddar cheese
½ cup reduced-fat shredded
    Monterey Jack cheese
1 medium tomato, diced
¼ cup chopped green onions

1. Preheat the oven to 375 degrees.
2. In a medium bowl combine the super-lean ground beef with

the flour, salt, minced onion, paprika, chili powder, garlic powder, and onion powder. Use your hands to thoroughly incorporate everything into the ground beef.

3. Preheat a skillet over medium/low heat and add the ground beef mixture to the pan along with the water. Brown the beef mixture for 5 to 6 minutes, using a wooden spoon or spatula to break up the meat as it cooks.

4. Spray both sides of each tortilla with a light coating of oil cooking spray. Place the tortillas onto baking sheets and bake for 10 to 12 minutes or until the tortillas are crispy and golden brown. Turn them over halfway through the cooking time, and pop any air bubbles if the tortillas begin to inflate. Keep the oven hot.

5. Heat up the refried beans in a small saucepan over medium/low heat, or in the microwave for 2 to 3 minutes, or until hot.

6. Assemble each pizza by first spreading about ⅓ cup of refried beans on the face of a tortilla.

7. Spread one-quarter of the meat over the beans.

8. Place on another tortilla, sandwiching the meat and beans between the two tortillas.

9. Coat the top tortilla with about two tablespoons of salsa.

10. Mix the two cheeses together and sprinkle about ½ cup over the top of the pizza.

11. Put a heaping tablespoon of diced tomato on next.

12. Garnish the pizza with green onion. Repeat the process with the remaining ingredients.

13. Bake the pizzas on a baking sheet for 8 to 12 minutes or until the cheese on top is melted.

14. Cut each pizza into quarters and serve hot.

• MAKES 4 PIZZAS.

Nutritional Facts (per serving)

SERVING SIZE—1 PIZZA   TOTAL SERVINGS—4

	LITE	ORIGINAL
CALORIES	427	570
FAT	10G	36G

•　　•　　•　　•

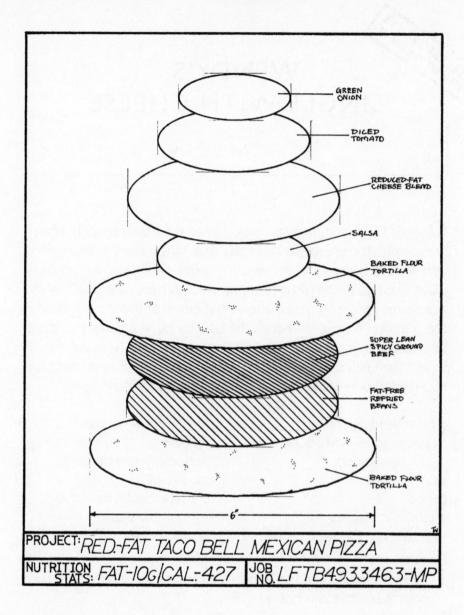

GREEN ONION

DICED TOMATO

REDUCED-FAT CHEESE BLEND

SALSA

BAKED FLOUR TORTILLA

SUPER LEAN SPICY GROUND BEEF

FAT-FREE REFRIED BEANS

BAKED FLOUR TORTILLA

6"

PROJECT: *RED.-FAT TACO BELL MEXICAN PIZZA*

NUTRITION STATS: *FAT-10g/CAL.-427* **JOB NO.** *LFTB4933463-MP*

WENDY'S
SINGLE WITH CHEESE

☆   ✌   💣   ✏   ◉   ✂   ☞

Over 5,000 Wendy's restaurants around the world serve the hamburger with the unique square patty that hangs over the edge of the bun. It's the burger that inspired the 1984 award-winning ad campaign that had a little old lady crying out, "Where's the beef?" With this secret recipe to create a lower-fat clone of the famous burger, the question is now, "Where's the fat?" By using super-lean ground beef, fat-free mayonnaise, and fat-free cheese, we have cut the fat to less than half of what is found in the original. Now you can have two cloned burgers for less than the fat found in one original.

1 plain hamburger bun	1 slice fat-free American
1/4 pound super-lean ground beef	cheese
(7 percent fat)	1/2 teaspoon yellow mustard
salt	1 lettuce leaf
pepper	2 to 3 separated onion slices
1 teaspoon ketchup	1 large tomato slice
1/2 tablespoon fat-free mayonnaise	3 dill pickle slices

1. Brown the faces of the bun in a large frying pan over medium heat. Keep the pan hot.
2. On wax paper, shape the ground beef into an approximately 4 × 4-inch square. You may find it easier to freeze the patty ahead of time, so that it doesn't fall apart when cooking. Don't defrost.
3. Cook the burger in the pan for 3 to 5 minutes per side, or until done. Salt and pepper both sides during the cooking.

4. Spread the ketchup and then the mayonnaise on the top bun.
5. Put the cooked patty on the bottom bun. On top of the meat, lay the slice of cheese.
6. Spread the mustard on the cheese, then place the lettuce, onion, tomato, and pickles on, in that order.
7. Complete the sandwich with the top bun and microwave the whole thing for 15 to 20 seconds to warm it up.

- SERVES 1.

Nutritional Facts *(per serving)*

SERVING SIZE—1 SANDWICH   TOTAL SERVINGS—1

	LITE	ORIGINAL
CALORIES (est.)	335	420
FAT (approx.)	10G	21G

• • • •

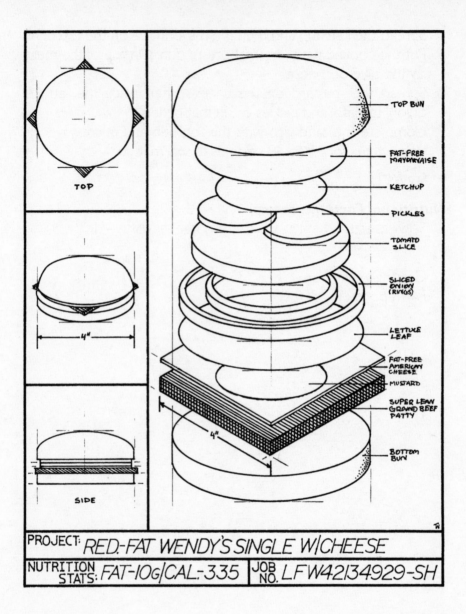

TOP

4"

SIDE

TOP BUN

FAT-FREE
MAYONNAISE

KETCHUP

PICKLES

TOMATO
SLICE

SLICED
ONION
(RINGS)

LETTUCE
LEAF

FAT-FREE
AMERICAN
CHEESE

MUSTARD

SUPER LEAN
GROUND BEEF
PATTY

BOTTOM
BUN

4"

PROJECT: *RED.-FAT WENDY'S SINGLE W/CHEESE*

NUTRITION STATS: *FAT-10g/CAL.-335*   JOB NO. *LFW42134.929-SH*

WENDY'S FROSTY

☆   ✌   💣   ✎   ☯   ✄   ☞

Over 22 million gallons of this frozen chocolate dessert are served at Wendy's each year.

To make a version of this tasty treat at home that reduces the fat by around 75 percent, you will just need some fat-free vanilla ice cream, Nestlé Quik, and low-fat milk. Oh yeah, and a blender.

¾ cup low-fat milk (2 percent)   4 cups fat-free vanilla ice cream
3 tablespoons Nestlé Quik

1. Combine all of the ingredients in a blender. Blend on medium speed until creamy. Stir if necessary.
2. If too thin, freeze the mixture in the blender or in cups until thicker.

• MAKES 2 DRINKS.

Nutritional Facts (per serving)
SERVING SIZE—1 16-OUNCE   TOTAL SERVINGS—2
    DESSERT

	LITE	ORIGINAL
CALORIES	470	440
FAT	2G	11G

• • • •

WHITE CASTLE CHEESEBURGERS

☆ ✌ 💣 ✏ 🎱 ✂ ☞

Some may call them "whitey one-bites." They're also known as "sliders," "gut busters," and "belly bombers." This 300-unit Midwestern hamburger chain celebrated its 75th anniversary in 1996 without much of a peep, and the company continues to stay impressively profitable despite its low-key marketing. The cooking technique is unique to the chain, because it involves steaming the ground beef patties. The minced onions are placed on the grill, with a beef patty on top. The steam from the grilling onions rises up through the five holes in each thin, square patty, allowing thorough cooking without having to flip the meat over.

Now you can use the same method, but with reduced-fat ingredients, to cook a reduced-fat version of one of the country's oldest burger creations.

1 pound super-lean ground beef (7 percent fat)	salt pepper
16 dinner rolls	16 slices fat-free American cheese
½ small onion, minced	

1. Prepare the patties by separating the ground beef into 16 1-ounce portions. On a sheet of wax paper, form the portions into square, very thin, 2½-inch patties. Using a small, circular object, such as a straw or the tip of a clean pen cap, create five holes in each patty. Make one hole in the center of the patty,

and four holes surrounding the first one, with each about half an inch in from each corner. Freeze these patties, still on the wax paper, until firm.

2. Toast the faces of the dinner rolls, either in a hot frying pan over medium heat, or under the oven broiler.
3. In a hot frying pan or skillet preheated over medium heat, arrange tablespoon-size piles of onions, 3 inches apart. Salt and pepper each pile of onions.
4. Spread the onions flat, and then place a frozen beef patty on each pile of onions. Salt each patty.
5. Cook each burger for 4 to 6 minutes. If you made the patties thin enough, steam from the onions will rise around the meat and through the holes in the patty, cooking the meat thoroughly without having to flip it.
6. To build each burger, turn the bottom half of a dinner roll over onto a patty, then hold it down as you scoop a spatula under the meat and onions, and turn the sandwich over onto a plate.
7. Cut a slice of American cheese into 2-inch-square portions and place a square onto the onions on the beef patty.
8. Complete the burger with the top half of the roll. Repeat with the remaining burgers, and serve hot.

• MAKES 16 BURGERS.

Nutritional Facts (per serving)
SERVING SIZE—2 BURGERS   TOTAL SERVINGS—8

	LITE	ORIGINAL
CALORIES	310	310
FAT	5G	17G

• • • •

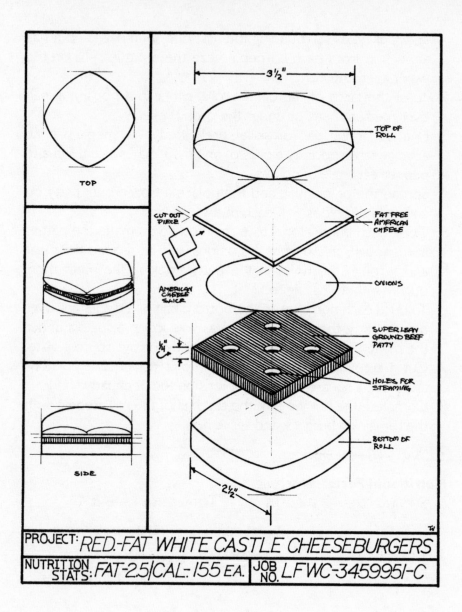

TOP

CUT OUT PIECE

AMERICAN CHEESE SLICE

SIDE

3½"

TOP OF ROLL

FAT FREE AMERICAN CHEESE

ONIONS

SUPER LEAN GROUND BEEF PATTY

HOLES FOR STEAMING

¼"

BOTTOM OF ROLL

2½"

PROJECT: RED.-FAT WHITE CASTLE CHEESEBURGERS

NUTRITION STATS: FAT-2.5/CAL-155 EA.

JOB NO. LFWC-345995I-C

TRADEMARKS

Applebee's and Low Fat & Fabulous are registered trademarks of Applebee's International, Inc.

Arby's is a registered trademark of Arby's, Inc.

Chili's and Chili's Guiltless Grill are registered trademarks of Brinker International

Einstein Bros. and Shmear are registered trademarks of Einstein Noah Bagel Corp.

Entenmann's and Entenmann's Light are registered trademarks of Entenmann's, Inc.

El Pollo Loco, B.R.C., Denny's, The Super Bird, and Moons Over My Hammy are registered trademarks of Flagstar Cos., Inc.

Gardenburger is a registered trademark of Wholesome & Hearty Foods, Inc.

Hostess Lights, Twinkie, Dolly Madison, and Buttercrumb Cinnamon are registered trademarks of Interstate Brands, Inc.

Kellogg's, Pop-Tarts, Rice Krispies, and Rice Krispies Treats are registered trademarks of Kellogg Company

Kraft, Kraft Free, and Catalina are registered trademarks of Kraft Foods, Inc.

Nabisco, SnackWell's, Golden Snack Bars, and Fudge Brownie Bars are registered trademarks of Nabisco, Inc.

Red Lobster, The Olive Garden, and Cheddar Bay Biscuits are registered trademarks of Darden Restaurants, Inc.

Swiss Miss is a registered trademark of Hunt-Wesson Foods, Inc.

INDEX